X-Ray

透 视 中 国

EXAMINING THE CHINA ENIGMA

©*Raymond Zhou*

CHINA INTERCONTINENTAL PRESS

图书在版编目（CIP）数据

透视中国：英文／周黎明著—北京：五洲传播出版社， 2008.5
ISBN 978-7-5085-1337-9

Ⅰ.透... Ⅱ.周... Ⅲ.文化-中国-文集-英文 Ⅳ.G12-53

中国版本图书馆 CIP 数据核字（2008）第 058007 号

X-Ray: Examining the China Enigma
by Raymond Zhou

Editor: Zhang Meijing
Book and Cover Designers: Miao Wei, Pan Hongwei and Du Yu
Illustrators: Zhang Yaoning, Luo Jie, Liu Yanfeng, Pang Li and Li Zhengming

ISBN 978-7-5085-1337-9

Published and Distributed by China Intercontinental Press
6 Beixiaomachang, Lianhuachi Donglu
Huatian Dasha, 24th Floor
Haidian District, Beijing, China
Post Code:100038
Telephone：58891280
Fax：58891281
http://www.cicc.org.cn

Layout and design: Beijing Jinxiushengyi Culture Development Company Limited C&C
JOINT PRINTING CO., (BEIJING) LTD

Printed by Beijing Youyi Printing Co. Ltd.
Format: 787 × 1092   1/16
Printed Sheets: 3000
First Printing: June 2008
RMB: 89.00 Yuan

Foreword

China Daily is blessed with some good writers and columnists: Some are Chinese with a world view; others are foreigners with global views of China.

But Raymond Zhou stands out — Chinese, yet an outsider who has studied and worked in the United States for 16 years, and brings a unique perspective to whatever he does.

He is the quintessential insider looking out; and the outsider looking in — without any emotional baggage.

His eclectic tastes — and specialties — are reflected in his writings: He majored in English language and Western culture from Hangzhou University and Sun Yat-sen University in China before being awarded an MBA from the University of California at Berkeley; he worked in capacities that promoted cultural exchange between China and the US; he is the most influential film critic in China, with a dozen books under his belt; he is considered a culture czar with a keen eye for art; featured across cultural platforms; and he is an avid fan of opera (both Western and Chinese) to boot.

Be they his much-commented-upon columns, his incisive commentary on social issues, his reports ranging from sociological matters to economic issues to travelogues where he paints a whole new face on a place, he has won over many.

What many readers enjoy — and appreciate — are his acute observations, empathy for his subjects and his pulse on the populace without ever being condescending.

Personally, I've enjoyed all his work. I'm sure you will, too.

I wish his endeavor all the best.

Zhu Ling

Editor-in-Chief

China Daily Group

CONTENTS

Chapter One
It's the Economy

1. Don't get carried away with GDP

August 04, 2007

China's economy will soon overtake Germany's, and by 2040 it will trump the US and become the world's number one.

That sounds like good news to me, but the euphoria over the prediction is nothing but unsettling.

The forecast is a slight variation of the ambitious scheme of almost half a century ago, namely, "overtaking Great Britain and the US".

You know how that one ended. But the ranking-conscious mentality is a reminder of how little we have matured even though our economy has made miraculous strides.

For one thing, GDP is only one barometer of an economy, and not a satisfyingly accurate one at that. It does not take into account the environmental cost and the psychological burden of torrid growth. That's why someone came up with the fuzzier "green GDP".

For another, GDP does not measure how each individual fares in an economy. When divided by 1.3 billion, we are still way behind and it's probably easier to count our ranking from the bottom up.

The irrational jubilation of some of my compatriots derives from a deep-seated insecurity, which is the result of a constantly refreshed memory of a century of the country's humiliation: We were beaten because we were weak. Now that we are strong, we can stand tall and proud.

There is nothing wrong with being proud of our achievement, but getting carried away with it may have negative consequences. Just as a nouveau riche may squander his money to boost his image and inflate his ego, a country has the same temptation. One seems to need a dose of superiority to overcompensate for the erstwhile sense of inferiority.

That is why it is extremely important to keep a clear head in a time of unprecedented boom and wealth. We need to focus on what should be done rather than gloating over what has been done. When you turn your sight from the metropolises to remote areas, you'll still be able to find poverty gnawing at a large swathe of our population. There are people who trek for half a day just to get a pail of water.

There are victims of natural disasters that need our help. There are countless people who toil under conditions that do not meet our stated or implied standards.

A surge in economic data is only meaningful when it benefits those who make it possible. GDP is just a number; it will have to be substantiated by things like better food on the table, roomier shelter for the family and more roads that link landlocked villages. It has to be made tangible with better and more affordable education, more and better-paid jobs, more choices of recreational activities, more access to information and more channels of expression.

If a higher GDP cannot be reflected in these things, why don't we just fill in whatever number we desire and be cheerful about it?

Along with great strength and stature comes great responsibility. Remember what Spiderman said? While a strong economy should improve the living standard of our populace, it also means we should spend more helping those in other countries who need help and join the international community in fighting Green Goblin, Doc Ock and Sandman – oops, I mean, terrorists.

A Chinese youth who thinks we can do whatever we want now that we will beat Germany and the US in GDP is playing right into the hands of those who advocate the "China threat". It's the flip side of " We were beaten because we were weak". But getting stronger does not necessarily mean acting irresponsibly. Let's start by acting rationally towards our progress.

2. Thou shalt not collude on pricing

August 20, 2007

Thou shalt not collude on pricing, the regulatory god said unto the Moses of industries in most countries, including China. But the instant noodle cabal either did not hear it or turned a deaf ear.

In late July, noodle makers joined forces in raising prices by about 20 percent, and as much as 40 percent for some products.

After less than three weeks of regulatory pressure, media assailing and public discontent, the industry backed down, apologized and initiated an across-the-board price cut.

Is this a triumph of consumer rights and regulatory protection?

Yes ... hmm maybe.

Instant noodle is more than the Chinese equivalent of the Western television dinner. The busy or lazy depend on it; the nation's gigantic floating population is buoyed by it; millions of train passengers slurp so many noodle cups that, if not muffled by the roaring locomotive, the collective giant sucking sound might be interpreted by space aliens as the whistle of earthlings.

The price upsurge was not unreasonable. Starting from late last year, cooking oil, a main ingredient, has been sizzling in price. Farm products such as flour, pepper and potato have all seen double-digit price growth. One media report put the average cost increase at 13-20 percent.

In face of shrinking profit, the biggest noodle makers called three meetings, discussed the situation and reached a consensus that affected 95 percent of the market. From their announcement, it could be viewed that they were proud of their concerted effort at deflecting a cost-induced crisis.

As one official put it, they have the right to raise prices, but no right to do it in accord.

Anyone with a modicum of MBA knowledge would know that. But it seems the notion that price-fixing was wrong did not occur to any of the participants, or they would not have trumpeted it.

Why didn't they know that their act would violate business regulations?

One reason could be there had been no such case before – not that there was no price-fixing before, but no prosecution of such cases.

So, why target the noodle makers? As ubiquitous as the product is, it is by no means an indispensable food item. There is no danger anybody would starve from a shortage of instant noodles as people can easily find substitutes.

The noodle makers are to be blamed in the first place because they did it with such high exposure that left regulators little choice but to handle the case by the book.

From another perspective, the noodle makers are really easy to pick on. Theirs is not a powerful interest group with close ties to the government. Their product is not so essential as to create a mass panic if thrust into market upheaval. In other words, they are the ideal "chickens" to be killed in order to scare the "monkeys". As a matter of fact, one economist used the same proverb to describe the nature of this story.

While it is certainly commendable that government agencies are pursuing violators of antitrust laws, we must go one step further and ask: What if it is an industry with which the government is financially entangled, such as the real estate business? What if it is an industry the government wants to promote and weed out the weaklings? And what if they all take cues from this case and change the tactics of price collusion from trade powwows to secret tête-à-têtes?

It would help create a healthy business environment if the noodle precedent is followed by more regular monitoring of the pricing practices of all industries, especially those that absorb a significant share of our income.

3. Can you monopolize song selection?

July 25, 2006

For those of you who frequent the nation's karaoke bars and lounges, what you sing will soon come under the centralized supervision of one really Big Brother.

Called "The National Karaoke Content Management Service System", it has been approved by the Ministry of Culture and will start a pilot program in three cities before it rolls out nationwide, according to the Chinese-language press.

The announcement of the news, attended by some Ministry officials, was made by the Culture Market Development Center, an organization under the Ministry. So far, the Ministry itself has refused press requests for confirmation or elaboration.

But the nation's business media has smelt a rat, so to speak.

"The Center is a '*guanshang*', a business run by a government agency, and it does not conceal its ambition to monopolize the karaoke market," says a commentary in Chinese Business View. "Even though it touts the principle of 'free choice to plug into the system', we have reason to worry that, with an entertainment platform built on monopoly, anything can happen."

The author of the article compares this system to China Union Pay, an electronic inter-bank system that started by offering "free lunch" and then graduated to a growing mountain of service fees, causing a major public outcry.

The "KTV tunes database", as the karaoke

system is known in layman's term, claims to have one major advantage in stamping out unauthorized use of copyrighted music: Every time a song is requested for singing-along, it will have an automatic record, and therefore, collect a royalty fee for the music label that owns its copyright.

In the past few years, music labels have occasionally targeted karaoke businesses for copyright infringement lawsuits. It is reported that no karaoke business in China pays royalties for every tune used. There is simply no such mechanism even if it wanted to.

The music labels have "expressed support for such a system", said a spokesman for the company that is building the system. But in recent interviews, some labels admitted that they did not really know how it would work out.

One more question: If participation is optional for a karaoke operator, why would he opt in and pay while his competitors can continue the free ride? Wouldn't that create an unfair environment for competition?

To my knowledge, this system by no means fills a void. There is an organization under the Music Association that is supposed to collect such fees. The dilemma is, it is incapable of enforcing the rules even when it wants to.

The most effective thing a centralized "KTV tunes database" can do is to filter out unwanted songs, as it states explicitly to be its top priority. But therein lies the biggest trap.

The database will forbid "unhealthy" songs from karaoke use. But who will define what is "unhealthy"? Some folk songs are quite racy by our standards, but they are part of the traditional dating rituals of some ethnic minorities.

And tastes change over time. Many of the love songs that we take for granted today would have offended millions had they appeared a decade ago.

Suppose the system errs on the side of precaution and goes for the "lowest common denominator". That would keep many of the unconventional tunes out of the door, especially rock, hip-hop and those created in Hong Kong and Taiwan.

It is no secret that many of the hot new melodies come from outside the mainland, where the pop music scene has a freer rein. The sensitivity displayed in those songs would no doubt offend some censors, who tend to have conservative tastes.

On top of it, there is the time lapse in okaying imported music in time for karaoke consumption. As most albums are released simultaneously all over Asia, a consumer who prefers "hot" tunes may not be able to find them in the "KTV database" as they bide their time in the pipeline of approval from censors, a scenario common with film imports.

If that happens, the karaoke business will be sapped of its vitality as it takes on an antiseptic feel. Songs pushed by the system may be those grandiloquent arias, while those giving voice to private feelings such as angst and frustration may be snubbed.

In the worst case, the grass-roots sing-along business may wither.

4. Pork price swing can be minimized

May 26, 2007

Pork is the talk of town.

In terms of the intensity of press coverage, it has overtaken real estate and almost rivaled the stock market as something that keeps rising and rising.

In the first three weeks of May, pork prices have increased greatly. In most cities, the price has doubled in the past year, making grocery shopping a very unpleasant experience of partial inflation.

Pig farmer

rice swings

Only a few days ago some commentators were trying to play this phenomenon down by quoting people who said a 17-percent monthly price hike wouldn't really "affect us". Now many are suggesting that the government take action to curb the price surge. You can literally see the tide of public opinion ebb and flow as whitewashers turned from being politically correct to politically incorrect.

A price change in a staple food like pork disproportionately upsets the poor, as more of their disposable income goes to these items. The incentive for government intervention is tempting. However, unlike the ever-rising housing market, there is little that can be blamed on the government here. It is mostly the market at play, the invisible hand that is pushing up pork prices.

The main reason for the price hike is that the price was too low last year, therefore many farmers lost money and decided to quit the business, combined with an epidemic that hit a vast swathe of the pig population. On top of that, feed prices have been going up. In Hunan Province, the heart of pig farming, 8 million fewer pigs were raised in the past year, severely draining supplies.

It is foreseeable that the pendulum will swing in the other direction in the future: in pursuit of fat profits, a lot of farmers will jump into the business, again creating a supply glut and driving down prices. This has been true of many agricultural products, including soybeans, peanuts and corn.

There is not much the government can do. The so-called reserve will just be a drop in the ocean. The pork reserve in Hunan translates into only 61,000 pigs, accounting for less than 1 percent of the shortfall. What's worse, there is a ripple effect. Vendors are nudging up the prices of other produce, such as eggs, beef and fish. This is the result of substitute shopping – buying something else when you wanted to buy pork, as advised by media experts.

The crisis will get worse before it gets better as the cycle of pig farming takes at least half a year. While no short-term solution can be expected, we can at least learn the lesson and be smarter next time.

Price swings for agricultural products cannot be completely eliminated, but can be minimized. Since pork consumption is not a wildcard, demand can be calculated with relative accuracy.

Normally, this should be the task of the pig farming industry. Because China's pig farmers are not organized, the government has the responsibility to provide such a service. Demand forecasts can be cheaply distributed through electronic media such as radio and television, which are all government-owned and controlled. The incremental cost is very low.

That leaves the collection and analysis of data, which can be time-consuming. But we have many colleges and institutes that study agriculture. They have a duty to care about such things as next season's pork price. They are all government funded and live on salaries. Why explore hypothetical problems when you can solve real ones?

Market research and forecasting is not a foolproof science, but it beats the wild fluctuations that result from chasing short-term profits. A healthy futures market can also modulate the fluxes.

It is telling that nobody is calling for government price control à la the old days. For all its deficiencies, a market economy is better than a command economy. Managed well, it can win the hearts of grocery-shopping grannies.

Note: Pork prices have not been stabilized yet. Some experts say the real culprit is rising energy prices, plus the demographic change of population flowing from pig-raising rural to pork-eating urban areas.

5. Food safety officials must be on alert

November 21, 2006

First it was eggs with red yolks, and now fish with thin, round bodies. It seems pretty things are not supposed to be put on our plates.

Only a few days ago, ducks in some parts of Hebei Province were found to have been fed a special red dye that later tested positive for carcinogens, so that their eggs would have red yolks. Compared with regular yellow-yolk eggs, these red-yolk eggs fetch a premium price in supermarkets and farmers' markets around the country.

Over the weekend, turbot fish sold in Shanghai were found to contain an element that causes cancer. They have been traced to fisheries in Shandong Province. Further testing revealed that fodder for the fish contained chemicals usually used to treat sick animals.

As one can expect, prices for turbot fish plummeted as authorities began inspections of other fisheries. But how can a grocery shopper be sure that the next food item they put into their basket is safe to eat?

The harmful eggs and fish were uncovered by random checks by the authorities or the media. While they deserve plaudits for these efforts, it is obvious that such sporadic safety checks, which are often clandestine in the case of media investigations, are not enough. There has to be a mechanism to make sure every food item sold is free from harm.

Of course it is unrealistic to test every egg or every fish. But the testing has to be so systematic and foolproof that greedy growers would not even think of using noxious ingredients in their feed. It is too late when inspectors go into overdrive after learning of incidents of mass poisoning or consumer complaints.

Theoretically we do have special departments dealing with food safety. But where were their eyes and ears when a reporter who visited a duck farm heard that farmers never eat their own poultry? Shouldn't that be a tip-off for a sign of dirty dealing?

Something as vital as food safety should not be left to the occasional prying of reporters, who usually do not have the resources or knowledge for this kind of thing. Don't get me wrong. They are doing a great service for public health. But think about it. If professional inspectors did a good job, reporters would not need to carry hidden cameras and smuggle samples to testing labs. If reporters are having a field day on food safety, it can be inferred that those who should do it as a full-time job have failed in the first place.

When a food poisoning scare breaks out, consumers consider themselves the victims, but producers – those law-abiding ones who do not inject their poultry or fish with chemicals - will be hurt just as badly, if not more. While the whole food category is banned and remaining products condemned, those whose livelihoods depend on it will take the heaviest toll as a result of the bad apples in their midst and the subsequent indiscriminate crackdown and mass panic.

First of all, laws should be scientific. For example, the SK-II scare, though not food-related, showed that laws have to specify the exact level that should not be exceeded by a certain component. The public should be aware that in the real world nothing is pure, and hazard ensues only when the object consumed reaches a certain quantity.

But more often, it is the implementation that should be improved. Unscrupulous merchants would do anything to make a quick buck, and officials protecting consumer safety should be on constant alert to new ways of tampering with products, especially food items, which affect virtually everybody.

It will be a sign of victory for food safety officials when reporters with hidden cameras have a hard time finding story leads for exposés on this topic.

6. Small things make up the big picture

July 14, 2007

The Qinghai-Tibet Railway has been open for a year now, but most passengers climbing up to the "Roof of the World" have opted to sidestep Xining, somewhat of a gateway to the plateau.

It is not because the capital of Qinghai Province does not have an abundance of tourism resources to offer. The culprit is scarcity of tickets from Xining to Lhasa, capital of Tibet Autonomous Region.

Once you get off at Xining and spend a few days taking in such sceneries as Ta'er Temple and Qinghai Lake, you'll probably end up stuck there. During the summer season, there is a daily demand for 1,200-plus seats originating from Xining, but only 700-some are available.

Don't even think about getting a seat on the other Lhasa-bound trains that depart from other cities and pass through Xining. They are all booked solid through the holiday season, which runs from June to October.

This has made the tourism bonanza elusive for Qinghai and also left a typical Qinghai-Tibet travel plan disappointingly incomplete for tourists.

Granted, there are reasons why the current capacity of 3,480 tickets to Tibet cannot be raised. Train cars used in the newly built section of the railroad have to meet stringent specifications for high-altitude operation, including pumping oxygen into air-tight cars. And unlike the packed-like-sardine trains elsewhere in China, no over-booking is allowed on this route.

While emphasis on passenger safety is commendable, the inflexibility towards market fluctuation is puzzling. During off season, trains run at only 50-60 percent of capacity.

A question arises: How come a railroad with such daunting engineering difficulties, including stretching across 550 km of permafrost, could be successfully built, but adjusting the number of trains to better reflect seasonal changes of the market appears to be so arduous?

I asked many railway authorities on my trip to Qinghai, but did not find a satisfying answer. Instead, they gave me the look as if I didn't know what I was talking about.

I often get this kind of perplexed look when I ask about annoyances in urban management. For example, the Capital Airport has a public announcement system so loud that it drowns out a cellphone conversation. Could they tune it so that it's clearly audible but does not simulate shouting? Does the system have only two volume levels – off and shrieking?

The same goes for the city's bus service. For a while, ticket sellers were alerting passengers to the name of the next bus stop. I asked one of them why they didn't use a recorder-speaker, and she replied that it would be "noisy to the residents in nearby buildings".

I guess a lot of people shared my curiosity. Soon, the speaker was back on. And now I can hear buses pulling in from my apartment 100 meters from the street.

I know bus announcement systems can modulate their volumes because I've seen buses in other cities with volumes just loud enough for the waiting passengers. The problem seems to be that those departments run by bureaucrats rarely pay attention to the small things in customer service.

Why should a train run with more cars in the busy season and fewer cars in the off season? Why should a bus or airport speaker be easy on the ear? These may not be life-or-death issues, but it is the job of management to find them out and calibrate for the best possible result.

Xining could increase the frequency of trains to Lhasa, but that would come after local government officials make multiple requests and possibly hold many coordination meetings. On most occasions, there must be mountains of complaints from the public before action is taken. When will the bureaucrat managers get proactive and resolve those minor troubles before they grow into an avalanche?

7. Reverse brain drain a sign of the times

December 16, 2006

As the saying goes in Journalism 101, when dog bites man, that's not news; only when man bites dog should a reporter jump on it.

Along the same lines, when farmers swarm into urban areas, it is more or less taken for granted; but when urbanites start settling down in the countryside – and not just for a holiday, that's newsworthy.

A recent report by China Youth Daily said as many as 5,000 university graduates, some from such prestigious institutions as Zhejiang University and Jiaotong University, had applied for rural residence permits in coastal Zhejiang Province, a prosperous area south of Shanghai.

That would have been unthinkable a generation ago. During the heyday of the Cultural Revolution (1966-76), urban youths were "sent down" to "remote mountains and countryside for re-education". As a way of solving unemployment, that didn't really work out well; but as a countermeasure for dealing with disenfranchised and rebellious youth, it hit a nerve, albeit inadvertently. The young were so eager to crawl back to their urban roots that the fight for a chance became the ordeal of their day, which, in turn, wised them up to the ways of the world and set them up for their future success.

The yawning urban-rural gap in China virtually amounted to a caste system. Those with urban residency used to be guaranteed jobs plus welfare, while those without had to make do with tilling a plot for life. About the only way to break through was by joining the army or going to college, after which one could possibly "convert" to urban status.

The "new educated youth", as the current batch is being nicknamed, differ from their predecessors in that they have been neither tricked nor had it drummed into them to downscale. Their decision to resettle in what was formerly considered the lower stratum was quite rational to begin with. It is the result of a push-pull convergence.

First there is the push from urban life – the scarcity of good jobs, the high cost of living and, above all, the prohibitive cost of housing. If a graduate hovers in the 1,000-2,000 yuan (US$127-US$255)

range of monthly earning power, they have little chance of becoming a proud city slicker.

The pull comes mainly from the ever-improving living standards and relatively low cost in some rural areas. Besides, with urbanization going strong as it is, rural land is skyrocketing in value. The plot for a homestead could sell for tens of thousands or even hundreds of thousands of yuan, which constitutes a windfall for most families.

It is a good sign that the brain drain is reversing. But we must realize that the reversal is just a trickle. The income gap between urban and rural citizens is far from being bridged. Rural life is getting better, that's for sure, but in many places the distance to the good life in the city is even farther than before.

Then, there is the residence permit system that holds migration in check. Although reform and opening up since the early 1980s has made it less relevant, it is not totally obsolete. For example, those returnees did not really move to other places; they were born and grew up there. Even they were granted special permission to go back to their native soil because land is now scarce and country folk do not want outsiders to carve up their "buried treasures", so to speak.

In other words, if you were born a townie, there's little likelihood you could opt for a bucolic country life. You can get a job there, but you cannot legally buy real estate or obtain permanent residence. You're just a member of the floating army, which now stands at 150 million.

So, what does this "man-eating-dog" phenomenon suggest? A new countryside taking shape? Possibly. More university graduates lacking competition in the concrete jungle? Could be.

More than anything, it tells us that, in a time of change, anything can happen. You never know where your next big break will come from.

8. 'Urban village' an eyesore in growth

Janary 14, 2006

The term "urban village" connotes very different things in English from what it does in Chinese.

In English, it usually refers to a well-planned development at the edge of an urban area. In the US, a residential "village" is called a "subdivision", with swimming pools and tennis courts, and rows of well-landscaped single-family houses.

In China, a *cheng zhong cun* (literally "village within a city") may be far from the skyscraper-crowded downtown, or it may lie in the shadow of the high-rises.

"Village" in Chinese often alludes to a farming community, and those urban villages that used to be farmland a decade or two ago. Hence the name. Now they are a major headache for urban planners across China, in big metropolises and small towns alike.

A typical urban village in today's China has absolutely no planning. The residents used to be farmers but now are mostly landlords and the majority of residents are migrant workers. The streets, if they can be called that, are narrow, dirty and lined with all kinds of small shops selling fake or shoddy merchandise. It's the birthplace of much of a city's sweatshops and crime cases.

Like bankrupt State-owned enterprises (SOEs), these villages are remnants of the old times, when urban planning was non-existent and suburban farmers scrapped a living from growing vegetables and peddling to city slickers. But unlike the SOEs, few solutions have worked.

If you demolish them without proper compensation, there will be unrest among the residents. If you pay market price, the cost will be prohibitive since urbanization has driven them into prime real estate. And since municipal governments can hardly afford the job, they'll hand it over to developers, who can be unscrupulous and ruthless in kicking out the original residents.

We have seen reports of these tragedies. But that's not the whole story. Sometimes it's the local government that is held hostage by greedy residents.

Some readers will ask at this point: "How can you take the side of the powerless and downtrodden in this kind of dispute? Where is your conscience as a journalist?"

If you dig deeper, you'll find that the victims of urban development are the urban poor, say, those with 20-square meters to a family. No matter how reasonably compensated they are, it's not likely they'll be able to live in their old neighborhoods any more.

However, the original suburban farmers, as a whole, profit extremely well from urban sprawl. Even though all land belongs to the State in name, they divvy up the money when the land, accurately speaking, the right to land use, is sold, generating hundreds of millions of yuan for a single small village.

These residents, in anticipation of big-money buyout, scramble to build all kind of structures on their plots so that when the city administrators come to measure their properties, they'll get more richly recompensed. In cities like Shenzhen or Guangzhou, the housing complexes they built have such narrow passageways that only one bike can go through them. Stairways are dark all day long and corridors are cramped and piled with all sorts of junk. Fire hazards are everywhere and there's little chance a fire truck could get close.

Suddenly awash with easy money, some of these landowners and sellers have turned to business ventures, but stories of gambling and drug binges also abound. A distant relative of mine died of overdose while squandering his "land money" on drugs. Some of his old neighbors are still spending their entire days on mahjong games.

Desperate for a way out, some cities have turned to consultants from Western countries. Surprisingly, these experts say: "Don't change a thing. This is how people live and interact. It reflects a lifestyle that should be respected."

So, are "urban villages" a cultural heritage or an eyesore? They are not on anyone's tourist routes, and the renting public inside them don't live there because they like to, but because they cannot afford a decent place.

Would a Western consultant say: "Don't clean up a slum because gentrification will change the way people interact?" Probably not. Allow me to be blunt: these "urban villages" are virtual slums.

The buck can indeed be passed to local governments, which did not have the foresight to properly zone suburban areas when they were still farmlands. Once migrants swarmed in, and stores and sweatshops sprouted up, it was too late.

Eventually the market may be able to take care of it when developers can offer a high enough price to buy up all the shanties and build something new and exorbitantly priced. Or they may – road conditions permitting – bypass these places and build out into the far suburbs, leaving pockets of unseemly blocks on the cityscape, a reminder of urban growth that is uneven and under-prepared.

Chapter Two
It Takes All Kinds

9. Names in stone mark much-deserved appreciation

January 21, 2006

In an act of powerful inspiration, a public library has carved on its wall the names of the construction workers who built it.

There are 626 names engraved on a white marble plaque displayed in the brand-new Hainan Province Library, divided into seven categories by the origins of their birthplaces: Hainan, Guangdong, Fujian, Jiangxi, Anhui, Sichuan and Hubei provinces.

It was a treatment usually reserved for inscriptions by senior officials and corporate names of architects and builders, or in Western countries, for donors whose money funded the building. But this acknowledged the blood and sweat of migrant workers who physically built the structure.

"They come from five lakes and four seas, but they are the heroes who have built up our province," gushed Chen Wendong, general manager of Hainan Construction Company. "When we urban dwellers enjoy the fruit of their hard work, we should not forget their contribution."

You can interpret it as grandstanding; you can even view the whole act as a symbolic gesture, which it in fact is.

But in this case, the symbol is powerful: The tens of millions of migrant workers who are shaping China's skyline with their hands should be treated with respect. It is especially urgent in a time when they are the most visibly downtrodden stratum of our society.

The Hainan authorities in charge of the project have gone beyond what they were supposed to do, which was to pay the workers properly and without delay.

"I participated in three construction projects in Hainan last year, but only the library did not owe me a penny," said Chen Tongxue from Sichuan, whose name is listed on the plaque.

At another job in Jiangsu Province, the defaulted payment for him and 279 of his co-workers ran up to more than half a million yuan (US$61,730). "We are laying the bricks and tiles for urban build-up, but it is hard to get the pay promised us. And now it is the end of the year again," he said.

The end of year on the lunar calendar is traditionally a time to clear all debt. It is also a time when some business operators in China, especially those in the construction industry, will go to extreme lengths to avoid paying their employees what has been contractually owed for months.

The marble plaque in Hainan Library cost some 100,000 yuan, but its value as a beacon of business ethics and decency is priceless. The latest reports show there are people visiting the library just to see the plaque and read the names.

There has always been something fetishistic about carving names in stones. Ever since the fictional Monkey King etched "I have been here", generations of Chinese tourists have followed suit and carved their names in the stones of the Great Wall and other historical buildings in a vain attempt to acquire immortality at the cost of defacing public properties.

Another fictional character, Willie Stark in *All the King's Men*, had a penchant to inscribe his name on all kinds of public structures. Based on real-life Louisiana Governor Huey Long, the protagonist of the Robert Penn Warren novel named a lot of things built during his reign after himself.

This is far from the worst offence for a politician. The man certainly had an oversized ego, but the projects seemed to serve public interests, at least the ones shown in the 1949 Oscar-winning movie version. He put up structures like bridges, which are not exactly white elephants, and more importantly, he did not pilfer public funds. (But then, he engaged in murder, which is a crime for any person.)

Officials deserve to have their names on public projects, which bring maximum benefit to local people and the officials are the single biggest force to make these projects possible. Isn't that better than spending the money on wining and dining? Then, the architect's name could be prominently displayed if the structure has the potential to be culturally significant.

To plaster hundreds of names of the people who actually build it, names that normally only the building contractor would have a record of, is not only unconventional, but has a touch of genius.

Now, it would take another genius to put up another plaque, in a conspicuous place, that inscribes the names of employers who treat migrant workers like dirt. Let's call it the "Wall of Shame", and I bet it would be an even bigger attraction.

10. Elevator ladies, checkout clerks and the human touch

November 26, 2005

"Why do you need elevator attendants?" a puzzled expat friend of mine asked shortly after he arrived in Beijing.

To an outsider, the person who operates an elevator – or lift in British English – may typify job redundancy. What on earth does it take to press a number that corresponds to the floor? What's the necessity for such a special profession?

I've also heard of complaints from expats who see these elevator ladies – it's a profession predominantly for females – as the personification of Big Brother. I don't know whether it's a thing of the past or the current situation as I have not met a nosy one myself. I'm sure I'd hate it if the elevator operators whom I come into contact with poke their noses into my comings and goings.

But no, those I've encountered are all nice and friendly. And come to think of it, they do perform a duty beyond that of pressing a few buttons. In a sense, they double as security guards. One example: Someone in my building had a broken lock and didn't bother to fix it, leaving his door unlocked for several months. I guess this would have been crazy in a building with unmanned elevators.

The real question is: For all the potential misgivings or benefits, shouldn't the profession be superfluous in the first place? Man designs machines to save manpower. In an economically efficient world, repetitive manual labor should best be performed by machines, leaving humans to more creative activities.

But we don't live in such a world, and sometimes economics is not the only law we should abide by. While it is the job of economists to study efficiency, the government needs to consider the broader human factor. A Beijing engineer once told me that many metropolises in China have done away with bus conductors, letting the driver oversee the automated depositing of bus fare. But not in Beijing, for the most part. The technology is available, but that would leave tens of thousands of low-skilled workers unemployed.

Now I'm no Luddite. Technologies have brought us an endless stream of wonders, making our lives easier and more comfortable. But the human cost of this kind of social advance is also real, especially to someone whose livelihood is threatened by it. As a society, we cannot shy away from taking these painful steps so that we can maintain our competitiveness and achieve progress, but at the same time we must always remember those who are negatively affected and ponder how to lessen their sufferings.

It is a delicate cost-and-benefit balance in not only economic – but also social – terms. A corporation needs only look at the bottom line, but a society at large needs to take care of the weak and disadvantaged. The "iron rice bowl" is indeed an impediment to progress, but designing jobs for low-skilled workers is not. On the contrary, it can create a higher level of harmony for our living environment. On a more personal level, it can add a unique human touch to things we take for granted.

When I first went to the United States, I marveled at the convenience of customer service via telephone calls. In the past 10 years, things started to change. The numbers are still toll-free, but you can hardly talk to a live person any more. Instead, you have to wade through a jungle of recorded prompts and choices and wait forever. Surely companies have cut cost as a result, but imagine the aggravation that customers must endure.

On recent trips, I have found that automation has taken a giant leap forward. Some supermarkets have removed not only baggers – those who place your groceries into bags, but also all checkout clerks. Now, I have to scan the packaged goods and weigh vegetables all by myself. I'm sure the process will be a breeze in the future, but the time I tried it I was so frustrated that I yelled: "I'm taking this out without paying if you guys don't show up now."

To those of us with memories of China before the reform years, the word "supermarket" already implies self-service. Do we need to eliminate checkout clerks so that we can save a penny on our grocery? Will haircuts be the only business that involves human interaction?

Nowadays, when I see retired people guarding busy street corners and directing traffic, a feeling of appreciation wells up: They are doing something worthwhile, not superfluous, for all of us, something that traffic lights are supposed to do, but not very well, during rush hours. They make Beijing a more livable city, at least traffic-wise.

Note: Beijing buses have since installed card reading machines, but ticket sellers have been kept intact.

11. Don't treat street vendors as the enemy

September 29, 2006

They hawk their wares on sidewalks, pedestrian overpasses or underpasses. They are the target of crackdown by *chengguan* (urban management authorities) and neighborhood complaints. They are China's street vendors.

The Cantonese call them "running ghosts" because they take off and vanish at the appearance, or sometimes just the sound, of *chengguan*. A more appropriate metaphor might be "running mice" as their trepidation is caused not only by "cats", those who can destroy them in one swoop, but by any "good citizen" who wants to report them. Technically, they are breaking the law and should not have any presence on our supposedly pristine urban landscape.

But finally, one person has given them some respect – a senior official of the Construction Ministry, no less. At a recent conference in Guangzhou, Vice-Minister Qiu Baoxing said our cities should have more tolerance for small peddlers and authorities should loosen restrictions at times such as weekends.

This reminded me of a poem I heard on the podcast "Antiwave". It tells of a street vendor's helplessness and pleas, moving me to tears.

First, let's count the reasons why they should not exist: They clog public walkways and constitute unfair competition with the stores they may block or that sell similar merchandise. They are not properly registered or licensed, and therefore do not pay their due of fees and taxes. Their hygiene standard for food items may be below par, and some may sell counterfeits.

Now for the reasons why we should not act like Inspector Javert in *Les Miserables*: At the social nadir, they try to scrape a living not by stealing or robbing, but by providing services of small value but much convenience.

For most of them, registering a formal retail operation is not really an option. Had they amassed the capital to rent a storefront or pay all the fees, they would probably have moved up the social ladder.

We sometimes stumble upon the *chengguan* quasi-cops who beat up these peddlers and smash their food stands. Recently, *chengguan* have been described as "psychologically disadvantaged" because they get into scuffles with peddlers and could get hurt. If they are "disadvantaged", would that turn the vendors into an "advantaged" lot? When you tear down their food carts and break their bowls and woks, it is their livelihood you are destroying.

I guess local governments are spending more money on these sweeps than vendors can make by selling hot potatoes or trinkets. Ironic, isn't it?

Do street vendors wreak havoc with our social and business order? Yes and no. They do create noise and crowds and litter the pavements, but they also add a sparkle to the vibrancy of a city scene and maybe even the seed of a future business segment. Some cities, in fact, have already realized this. It was reported that in a city in Shandong Province, vendors are allowed to do businesses in residential areas and in non-major streets.

Many of China's giant wholesale hubs started some 25 years ago as such street ventures. My hometown had strict rules and stricter enforcement, driving most of the early peddlers out of town. The next town was more laissez-faire. As a result, it now has a "pillar industry" built on this cluster of erstwhile street entrepreneurs.

It is time our urban managers adjust their conception of what makes a city tick. We need gleaming towers of name-brand companies, but we also need small merchants who make the wheel of business run more smoothly. In the same vein, we need street performers as well as gilded theatres.

That does not imply there should be no regulation on street vending. For one thing, food safety should be taken seriously. They may not be hustling ginseng soup, but whatever they sell should not be a hazard to whoever buys it. And the vendors should clean up after themselves, which will not add to their financial burden. When a cluster forms and business booms, the successful ones may be enticed to move into a sheltered space, and eventually to shopping malls.

Meanwhile, locations for street peddling should be managed so that vendors can profit from traffic flows, yet will not negatively affect the surrounding area.

Most importantly, charge reasonable fees – fees that reflect their earnings and are commensurate with the services our urban administrators offer. And by "services", I do not mean wielding one's fists or batons or impounding or trashing merchandise.

As for us urban dwellers who may be inconvenienced by the vendors, put ourselves in their shoes and show some understanding and tolerance. That's what a harmonious society takes.

12. Schlepping for a little respect

May 12, 2007

A week ago, some 30 college students from Southwest University of Political Science & Law spent a Golden Week day doing something they would never want to do unless it was part of a school project.

They joined the "pole army".

Cutely known as "*bangbang* army", its ranks are made up of migrant workers with shoulder poles. They are as integral a part of Chongqing Municipality as tourists are to the Forbidden City. Because the hilly terrain of the city presents a problem for motor traffic, these workers help carry groceries and other stuff for residents who have to climb up flights of steps to reach their homes.

They are at the bottom of the pecking order. For these students, it was a simulation of life as it could have been – if they hadn't studied hard and gotten into college, that is.

To get business, many of them cut prices so low that they ended up earning only 1 yuan for a whole day. One of the law students was visibly shaken. His parents are in real estate, giving him a monthly allowance of 3,000 yuan. On that day, his sweat brought him only 1 yuan.

I assume the organizers had something else in mind. They may have wanted the students, who will probably go into politics and law after graduation, to understand the hardship of the disenfranchised and the downtrodden, so they would speak for their rights upon graduating into positions of power. The immediate effect is that the students will work harder and get as far away from the lower depths of society as much as possible.

Last year, US Senator John Kerry told a group of college students that they could either work hard in school or "get stuck" in Iraq. The joke was designed to target President George W. Bush and his Iraq policy, but the implication is that those in the military are somehow uneducated, which "is insulting and shameful", as Bush criticized.

Similarly, according to the politically correct principles of the Chinese social mandate, we interpret physical work in only a positive light.

In the aftermath of the May 4th Movement, there was a concerted effort to glorify machine operating and farm tilling. Some 40 years ago, millions of urban youths were "sent down to remote mountains and countryside for reeducation". People went happily, waving flags and singing. But they found they weren't exactly in for camping trips. Many lamented their lost youth, although many have also

discovered and developed positive values from their grueling experiences.

One cannot create a class-free society by extolling physical labor or forcing people into it. Even the term "sent down" implies inequality.

The cold truth is, industrialization has rendered obsolete most forms of physical labor. And whatever remains will be handled by those with little or no job skill. The value of work is no longer measured by the sweat you shed, but rather, by the brain cells you put into it. A worker who uses his body as a tool of transport is worth less in economic terms than one who operates a truck, who, in turn, is worth less than the one who designed it. That's the economic reality, and it applies everywhere.

However, it is morally wrong to look down upon those who engage in backbreaking labor. As a society, we should find ways to improve the economic value of their work by providing job training. As we look up at the skyline and see the glittering skyscrapers, we should take off our hats to their builders, even though nobody would want to be one if he has a better opportunity.

13. Birth place no yardstick for place of death

April 28, 2007

On April 23, a speeding bus plunged 13 meters off the ramp of a bridge in Southwest China's Chongqing Municipality, killing 26 of its 32 passengers. Shortly afterwards, Deputy Mayor Zhou Mubing announced that compensation will be doled out regardless of the victims' residence status and a higher yardstick would be used in case of discrepancies.

Chongqing is possibly the world's largest municipality, encompassing large swaths of rural areas. It is reasonable to assume that victims include both urban and rural residents. By "urban" and "rural", I mean the residence permits people hold, not necessarily where they actually live. Migrant workers may work in cities for years, but legally they are not residents.

This is essentially a caste system that condemns a vast majority of the nation's citizens to a secondary status, with no safety net of insurance, healthcare or welfare to fall back on. Education is way below the urban standard, and salary-earning jobs are virtually non-existent.

This discrimination extends to the afterlife, so to speak. According to the current regulation, compensation rates are calculated by the average per-capita disposal income of the town, if the victim is a city slicker, or the average net income in the case of a rural resident. Since urban income is much higher, an urban resident, even when killed in a traffic accident, can command far higher compensation.

As revealed by Li Yuling, a member of the Chinese People's Political Consultative Conference, using the 2005 rates, the urban-rural gap for such compensation is 98,000 yuan ($12,700) in Sichuan, 110,000 ($14,300) in Hubei, 130,000 ($16,900) in Hunan, 140,000 ($18,200) in Jiangsu.

It is by no means a revelation that the rural population suffers discrimination. It is the ultimate insult when a life tragically cut short is worth so much less because that person was born in the "wrong" place.

To be fair, the force of reform unleashed by Deng Xiaoping has chipped away some of the shackles that used to chain rural residents to the land. Nowadays they can choose to work in cities, albeit under abominable conditions, and even buy real estate in places where they don't hold a residence permit, even though their children have to pay extra fees to get into public schools.

Ironically, people who advocate equal rights for rural residents are mostly urbanites with good education and a strong sense of right and wrong. In the public arena, rural people don't really have a voice. While it is admirable that we urbanites relentlessly highlight the woes of our rural brethren, some resort to an idealistic scenario in rebutting the old argument that repealing the residence system will cause havoc.

I have no doubt that a sudden surge of rural-to-urban migration in the absence of a two-tier system will exacerbate public security problems in our cities in the short run. Would you be surprised that a significant amount of urban crime, especially petty theft, is committed by rural migrants? We don't need to make the disenfranchised into saints to prove the system wrong.

The forecast of the authorities is correct because, by removing obstacles to the free flow of humanity, the negative consequences of urbanization will surface. But it is a moral issue that overrides the security issue. It is simply reprehensible to hold down one section of the citizenry so that another can enjoy more rights and government management will be easier.

The Chongqing municipal government is following several provinces in the right direction. It may not deliver the coup de grâce to this inherently iniquitous residence system, but any dent will help to dismantle the entrenched notion that everyone is equal but urbanites are more equal than country folks.

14. News on the move

Those of you who drive your cars or take public transport in Beijing don't know what you're missing. You're missing one of the city's top 10 attractions and an intangible cultural heritage that costs little.

Of course, nobody has conferred that title on Beijing's taxi drivers, but I would like to nominate them if such a category existed.

Taxi drivers in China's capital city are in a league of their own. I'm not talking about their driving skills or their knowledge of the city's roads, which doesn't seem to require more than one day's familiarizing. It is the rich mix of news and views that they offer – at no extra charge – that makes them stand out and add such joie de vivre to this metropolis.

True, New York has equally garrulous taxi drivers, but they tend to be new arrivals from one region – South Asia – at least when I was there 10 years ago, that may limit areas of interest for conversation.

Beijing taxi drivers are not only willing – at the slightest prompting – to open their chatterbox, but offer a spectrum of topics wider than some universities' curricula. They range from international politics to the latest gossip on the street. On a recent ride, I was given a lesson in linguistics, specifically, on the origin and connotation of "*peng ci'er*", literally meaning "to touch porcelain".

It refers to a form of petty extortion when some pedestrian deliberately walks into a car, usually one that has stopped at a traffic light, and pretends to be hit by it, thus claiming injury. The driver, unclear about his or her own culpability and eager to avoid making a scene, usually has to shell out several hundred yuan as settlement.

Now, no professor or dictionary could have taught me that. Besides, it gave me a glimpse of the shifting relationship between drivers and pedestrians in this city. A decade or two ago, when personal vehicles were far and few between, it would have been unimaginable for a pedestrian to come up with

such a scheme.

I jokingly call Beijing taxi drivers "my news agency on wheels". The information that I get on each ride is surely not edited by professional newsmen, but refracted through the prism of personal observation and imagination, or, shall I borrow a Hollywood term, re-imagining. It is somewhat like van Gogh's rendition of sunflowers – distinctive, whimsical and never boring.

If a topic is hot or controversial, you would get so many different interpretations that will set your mind in a spin. Early this year, I quizzed a dozen drivers on their takes on Sino-Japanese relations, and guess what? It was neither emotional nor rational. There were arguments that no foreign relations expert could have anticipated.

I always wonder why taxi drivers are inclined towards conspiracy theories. Somehow, they can connect the dots that are invisible to most of us and make the farfetched sound plausible. But they do give me pause for second thought.

I once met an elderly driver who gave me a scathing review of what he went through in the old days when Big Brother was running amok. I tantalized, "Back then, if you had told me this and I had reported it to your employer, you'd be in big trouble." He kept silent, and then said, "Times have changed and now I can confide in a stranger without fear."

Here's my taxi interview routine: as soon as I'm snugly in the back seat, I'd go, "Hey, *shifu* (usually translated as 'master' but more like a respectful 'sir'), what's new in this town?" as if I'm fresh off the train. And he'd – it's usually a he – delve right to the top story in the most journalistically correct way, never wasting time on sugar-coating generalities. The language is not something The New York Times would accept, but something Hollywood scriptwriters would die for.

I would refrain from giving him my employer's address as the destination. Instead, I'd mention the school across the street or even a nearby restaurant. Maybe, subconsciously, I do not want him to know I'm a journalist. Maybe I'm afraid the revelation might embarrass him, or maybe I'm the one who's a little embarrassed.

Chapter Three
Inside the Red Compound

15. Oath taken with a pinch of salt

August 19, 2006

Last Sunday, 500 newly recruited civil servants participated in a ceremony in Guangzhou. They all come from government customs and tax departments, which are deemed "highly vulnerable to corruption". (Actually, the original term is "highly dangerous professions", something that usually refers to construction workers who toil on skyscrapers, nurses who handle contagious diseases and the like.)

Wearing brand-new uniforms, they pledged to "work with loyalty and dedication, abide by the constitution and the laws, execute authorities conferred by the State, refrain from abusing power or seeking self-interest, be supervised by the masses and act as good public servants."

These are indeed noble and high-sounding words. But the problem is, are they useful in holding down the beast of corruption?

Some media commentators praise the oath as a psychological warning. One of the oath-takers told the press that he would think twice before getting into something murky: "I've made a pledge and it has got to have some restraint on me." Others say this is all pomp and protocol. "The motive is good, but I seriously doubt its effectiveness," reads an article in China Business Times. Many reports listed such ceremonies across the nation and concluded that the public has yet to see the effect.

It is sad that a pledge to resist corruption is automatically met with skepticism and derision. But it shows how widespread and taken for granted corruption is in our society. There was a time when most took such promises seriously. But like it or not, we have moved from "the Age of Innocence" into "the Gilded Age."

That is the breeding ground for cynicism. What used to be solemn and sincere words now sound bombastic at best and downright hypocritical at worst.

Despite good intentions, many of the rituals held sacred by the old generation do not apply in this time and day. People demand accountability. A pledge against corruption is nice to start with, but what

really matters is a mechanism, something like Hong Kong's ICAC, that reins in behaviors that constitute corruption and punishes officials for such wrongdoings.

Whatever positions they occupy, officials are first of all human beings and, like everyone else, have weaknesses when confronted with temptations. There are people who can rise above the hanky-panky a little longer, but without checks and balances, anyone is prone to straying from the rules if the rules are not enforced in the first place.

To chalk it up to character failings is an oversimplification and will only shift the focus from where it should be. And seeking to counter the complexity of human behavior with banal slogans is like the proverbial effort to put out a big fire with a cup of water.

The oath-taking ceremony is just a form. It becomes an empty pledge when not backed up with actions, and a laughingstock when blatantly contradicted by reality.

But even the ceremony should not be overdone. By its nature, ceremonies are already enhanced for dramatic effects. Overacting will only make it cheesier.

Some suggest that the young tax and customs officers may be sincere in their pledges. They haven't had the chance to embezzle or receive bribes yet. If the same ceremony is held for those who've already been in powerful positions for years, that will be either high drama or high camp.

16. Sadly, there is an Ah Q in all of us

July 15, 2006

A recent press report quoted a contractor by the name of Fang who had to bribe government officials for business opportunities.

In the interview he said: " Whenever I pass a bundle of cash to them, I see them as a useful dog that runs errands for me. Otherwise, I cannot keep myself psychologically balanced. Why should I stash their pockets with my hard-earned money and humiliate myself in the process? That money is my sweat and blood."

That is certainly one way of looking at it.

The officials on the receiving end of his "generosity" probably see themselves as well-deserving of such largess. "I provide you with a valuable service. Western firms pay hefty consulting fees, you know," they might reason. Or they might be more blunt: "I control the survival of your business. So you've got to pay up!"

For those of us outside this circle of corruption, Briber Fang is resorting to the classic approach of "mental victory", searching for a way to come out on top from the position of a victim. But don't accuse him of being self-delusional. It is a trait that has been associated with Chinese resilience.

The archetype of Chinese-style "mental victory" is the fictitious Ah Q, from *The True Story of Ah Q*, arguably the best literary work of 20th century China. As created by Lu Xun, this ordinary peasant is absolutely at the bottom rung of the social ladder. Landlords beat him up; women reject him. If he had any sense of objectivity, he would have been drowned in self-pity. But hell, no! He always gives the most positive spin on any hostile circumstances: Beaten by someone rich and powerful? Then Ah Q would mutter: "It was son beating father," as in Chinese hierarchy Father lords over Son. Rejected by the woman who caught his fancy? Then she is ugly, as demonstrated by her unbound feet.

We tend to view Ah Q as a clown, but there is an Ah Q in all of us – or he wouldn't be the archetypal Chinese. If we face an oppressive force, we call it the "servant" and see ourselves as "master" .

There is an adage that I heard when I was a kid: "If you profit from politics, you can last only 30 years; but if you make your living on a farm, you can last 10,000 years."

I don't know whether mandarins or peasants or scholars came up with this. But it was certainly designed to make peasants feel good about themselves. Of course a peasant's "career" lasts forever. Nobody wants to be a peasant because they are exploited by all other social strata, including us urban dwellers who pay them pocket change for backbreaking work.

When Lu Xueyi, a social scientist, came up with a new classification that divided the current Chinese society into 10 categories, those who found themselves in the lower rungs were not pleased: "We are supposed to be the masters of our society."

"But sorry, we determine the ranking by the resources and clout that a social group commands," explained the venerable professor.

Self-value is often crystallized into labels. But labels can be deceiving, and they can be out of date. For example, college graduates are the "proud sons of heaven". But if you know you are one of four million per annum, your pride will be hurt a little. And if you have ever jostled in a job market, you may feel downright miserable.

But the Chinese are not the only sons and daughters of Ah Q. If you've read *Harry Potter*, you'd know that the magic wand is simply a tool for mental victory. If you cannot beat up your evil cousin, just wish that he would fall into a snake pit. In reality, the evil cousin probably turns out to be a banker and Harry ends up working as a teller in one of his branches.

Just kidding. But that would be more auspicious than the fate of Ah Q, who wants to join a revolution but ends up losing his head on the execution ground. That's not something they teach at Hogwarts.

Before you call me a cynic, I'll say that there's nothing wrong with a healthy dose of chimera. In this upwardly mobile culture, not everybody can be a winner. Instead of hating yourself over losing, why not take an alternative view of it?

And for Briber Fang, don't abuse our favorite pet by associating it with corrupt officials. Maybe you can see your "gift" as a business expense. That'll make you feel better but less Ah Q-ish.

17. Slap on the wrist not enough for lying officials

November 25, 2006

Two months ago, Ye Dachuan told a visiting delegation that the city of Liupanshui had been "steady in maintaining grade-two air quality all year around", ranking it "the best in Guizhou Province". Besides, "there is no coal and chemical plant in its area of jurisdiction and no industrial enterprise in the area protected for water resources."

This sounded like a nice statement from a deputy mayor to the inspection team dispatched by the State Council. However, the inspectors didn't buy it and instead conducted an on-site investigation.

They found that the city had launched a power station project without due process; there were hazards of water pollution, even for drinking water; and there were more than 30 coking plants in operation.

The result was astounding not only because of the severity of the pollution, but because of the brazenness of Deputy Mayor Ye's lies. To borrow a sentence from Mark Twain: "No high-minded man, no man of right feeling, can contemplate the lumbering and slovenly lying of the present day without grieving to see a noble art so prostituted."

Indeed, this is an ideal illustration of the "decay of the art of lying". The master satirist would certainly have put Ye in the category of "ignorant uncultivated liar".

I'm not trying to justify what Ye did by suggesting that it was only how he did it that was wrong. As every kid knows while growing up, it is morally unacceptable to tell lies.

Unfortunately, we do not live in a kid's world. There are occasions when almost everyone has to be economical with the truth. But most people do distinguish between white lies that are meant to prevent embarrassment and vicious lies that are meant to harm.

I guess Ye did not intend to harm anyone deliberately, but by withholding the truth from higher authorities he thwarted their efforts to correctly gauge the environmental damage in the city and therefore to make policies and take measures to minimize it. As a direct result of his misrepresentation, the city's people would be hurt.

It is obvious that he lied for selfish reasons to shirk responsibility and keep his official position. But lying is not restricted to one occupation or one culture. The executives at Enron cooked the books and fleeced shareholders of billions of dollars. I dare say that when the temptation is big enough, most people would fall prey to it, and they would comfort themselves with all kinds of excuses.

That's why there should be a mechanism in place to curb government officials or officers of public companies from attempts at fabrication, and there should be a punishment for those who engage in it. Jeffrey Skilling, the former Enron CEO, got 24 years in jail. But Ye got little more than a slap on the wrist when the Ministry of Supervision and the State Environmental Protection Administration openly reprimanded him.

That is certainly a good start. But it will have some side effects, among which will be the elevation of "the art of lying". Saying black is white will be phased out, and quibbling will be in. If a public relations consultant gets involved, Ye would probably use words to the effect of, "Yes, we have problems, but things are improving."

By that time it'll require greater skills for us to read between the lines and figure out what the "problems" really are and how grave they are. But for the time being, government inspectors and statisticians have to make sure that facts are not distorted beyond recognition and data are not tailor-made to fit a picture-perfect design.

A quarter of a century ago, there was a stage play about an impostor who went around the country impersonating the son of a senior official. When he was arrested, he asked: "Would I have been a con man if I were indeed that person?" One thing is for sure: He would not have got the breaks he had.

Likewise, we must ask: What would have happened to the deputy mayor if he had been frank about the city's environmental woes? If he were commended for speaking the truth – it is another matter whether he was responsible for causing the damage in the first place – he might have no need to resort to deception.

18. 'Shameful' exhibition backfires

February 03, 2007

What do you call an auction where the sellers are hush-hush but the buyers enter into a bidding spree?

A marketer's dream, maybe. In the over-commercialized society that is today's China, businesses have to scream at the top of their voices to advertise themselves, but even that may not guarantee a significant turnout of customers.

A recent auction in Hefei, Anhui Province, attracted hundreds of buyers, who paid premiums as much as dozens of times over the listed prices of the items. The cash was meant for the cachet that the items carried with their previous ownership. They belonged to former governor Wang Huaizhong, former Fuyang mayor Xiao Zuoxin and five other deposed bureaucrats.

The officials were found guilty of corruption, and the items were seized as goods that they received as bribery. The filthy lucre was intended as a kind of "educational display" – a deterrent for the potentially bad apples among public servants. But judging by the feedback, it had the opposite effect.

A calligraphy couplet started at 50 yuan ($6), but was eventually sold for 3,200 yuan ($412). An imperial edict by Qianlong (1711-99) started at 100 yuan ($12), and ended up selling for 4,200 yuan ($520). Even a broken jade bracelet, something that would be thrown out as garbage, was snapped up for 10 yuan (50 US cents).

According to reports, the buyers were collectors and businessmen.

The irony was that many of the businessmen said they were scouting for gifts for officials. "The holiday season is coming, and we have to do something to help our business dealings," said one. In other words, the booty was being recycled – again used as inducement for official favors. What made them think that the 676 items of loot were great gift-giving ideas?

For one thing, they were less likely to be forgeries. Who would dare to give a fake Da Vinci, figuratively, for a license, an approval or an opportunity on which he stakes his future fortune? So, the quality of the arts, antiques and artifacts on offer was more secure.

There was also some value accumulated from the status of the previous owners. A painting may be worth 10,000 yuan ($1,200), but since Big Shot XYZ had it for a while, it now has a back story, an enriched history, so to speak. Now that some of the owners have been executed or are serving long prison sentences, that story has a layer of added drama and excitement, enhancing its curiosity value.

This reminds me of the "Red Mansion" in Fujian, the entertainment venue that uber-corrupter Lai Changxing used to seduce power players with beautiful wine and more beautiful women. The name took on such a mystique that some tourists would seek it out while traveling in Xiamen. If the local authorities had designated it as a tourist site, it could have generated revenues.

But people expecting an opulent palace were disappointed. The exterior of the building was subdued because the Great Smuggler did not want to attract attention. In a sense, this landmark of extreme corruption is no different from the Forbidden City, where royal families did not really separate state assets from personal belongings. If Lai had harbored any artistic ambitions and hired an architectural genius for the design, his "mansion" may well have become a similar site of "historic interest".

However, the government's intention of turning this and other loot into symbols of disgrace obviously did not work. As it stands, people were not dissuaded. Rather, they gauged the price of taking bribes whether it is worth the risk to take, say, a 65,000-yuan Rolex.

The biggest irony, though, is the cruel fact that many of the items have indeed been found to be forgeries. In the tug of war between money and power, a bribe may well be a replay of *The Necklace*, the poignant story by Guy de Maupassant.

19. Unconscious reflections of official mind

June 23, 2007

On a recent day, when a reporter dropped in on an office in North China's Shanxi Province, he found a group of people playing cards. It was during office hours.

This was not just any office, but the disciplinary committee of Hongdong County. Hongdong, if you have a one-week-long memory, is the epicenter of the scandal that shocked and shook the nation with its illegal kilns that enslaved mentally handicapped and under-age workers and treated them with unspeakable cruelty. It is the target of a campaign directed from the central government to free every slave and bring those responsible to justice.

In other words, this is probably not the best time for Hongdong officials to wind down and have a little fun. But of course they can justify it: they had been working overtime for the previous two days and needed a little rest.

Who can begrudge them some freedom from the sudden overload of outsider-induced drudgery? If they were fed only a few steamed buns and water a day, they'd be like the child laborers and want to run away. In an ironic similarity, one of the officials did escape from the window when a reporter guarded the door with a slew of questions.

Compared with the enormity of the kiln story, inopportune card-playing is just a minor act of insensitivity, hardly a sin among certain people.

Unlike most people whose indignation was raised another notch upon hearing this incident, I have been trying to make light of it. Think of it as stoicism in the face of unwanted media avalanche. To these people, life must go on. What's the point of putting on a sad face for the outside world when you can be yourself?

Between genuine numbness and hypocrisy, I may indeed prefer the former. That gives me less false hope. Whatever you may accuse them, these people are not guilty of fake compassion.

I bet as they learn the ways of the world they'll pick up all those tricks, and eventually, nobody – not even they themselves – will be able to tell whether they really feel your pain or are just play-acting. They may call it discomfort and we may call it progress.

Sometimes the most dramatic incrimination comes from those incriminated. But it took me a while to reconcile with the comically enlarged evidence. Outside a big bank in San Francisco, there is a black sculpture shaped like a heart. One day, a friend told me it represents the heart of a banker.

This line of reasoning opened my eyes to a new way of interpreting unhappy sights. When a television news anchor is repeatedly awarded, many audience members are pissed off because he always wears a smirk on his face. But you know what? This could be what his boss wants him to convey to his audience. Now I see him as very real while those with forced smiles give me goose-bumps.

It doesn't take a psychoanalyst to know that the subconscious seeps out from layers of protocol. Several county-level governments have built mansions that are not-so-faint reminders of the Tian'anmen Rostrum. It's not far fetched to interpret that they want to be emperors in their jurisdiction. If they had a choice, they would don the traditional garb and throw death warrants down to the floor as in those period dramas.

Efforts to bring governance up to par with our modern society are necessary and should be done on a systematic level. But for many local officials, it takes longer to change the mindset that they are not put in a place to thunder out proclamations like Moses, but to serve the people even when you want a moment of relaxation.

20. The 'rats' just keep nibbling

May 24, 2007

It may be the most powerfully suggestive detail of a toothpaste commercial: After trumpeting all the benefits of a brand, the advert closes with the stamp of approval from an authoritative organization called *Ya Fang Zu*, the Chinese acronym for the National Tooth Health Protection Group.

Imagine the shock when the Health Ministry dismantled the group, which the Chinese press described as "one table and two people". Actually, it had a staff of six people and has raked in 27 million yuan ($3.37 million) since its inception in 1997. The surprise is that its certification was not legally binding and the group itself was not even a legal entity. The non-surprise: Much of the money went into staffers' own pockets.

Mind you, this was not the brainchild of some scam artist. It was indeed affiliated with the Health Ministry, but not exactly a department of the ministry.

It is reported that P&G donated 10 million yuan ($1.3 million) to the group in 2002. The multinational company later explained that the money was meant for the namesake foundation and had nothing to do with the certification of its toothpaste.

Whatever the truth, the pattern is clear: A government-endorsed agency uses its power – power that is ultimately derived from taxpayers – to enrich itself rather than serve the public.

Suffice it to say, *Ya Fang Zu* was not the only offender, maybe not the worst either. The incremental cost to the consumer is so negligible that most people would never have given it much thought.

But there are so many agencies like that in China that they constitute a major burden on the economy. Take the real estate sector. Before ground is broken, the builder needs to get approval from dozens of government agencies. The process involves paying the nominal fee and, very often, a much higher charge in the form of a bribe or a coerced donation.

On top of that come the greedy developers, who add their obscenely fat margins. No wonder housing prices are as high as those in countries where per-capita GDP is 10 times higher than China.

Healthy Teeth

Consumer

A friend who is a college president told me he had to get an approval letter stamped by 100 different agencies before the college could build something on its campus. And a college is not a business, at least not in name.

That is why officials are adamant in opposing any measure that will require real estate developers to disclose their cost structure.

A senior official in the Northeast recently told me that, in an effort to build affordable housing for the poor, he pressured all agencies to waive their fees. Eventually he was able to lower the cost to 600 yuan ($75) per square meter. As a result, even the poorest of the urban poor could afford a decent unit.

Each of these agencies is supposed to provide a service. But shouldn't we ask how many of these services are really necessary and how many have evolved into get-rich-quick schemes that harm the public more than help it?

For example, food inspection is extremely important. Yet it is not uncommon for inspectors to descend on a farmers' market only to collect their fees. Any inspection they conduct is haphazard, driven by so-called campaigns – meaning when their boss is checking on them.

If you compare the cost of a restaurant meal in China with one in a Western country, you will find that miscellaneous fees levied by the government make up a much bigger share here. This may not be alarming when the economy is running full steam ahead, but it will drain our competitiveness. In a classic poem, these fee collectors are called "rats" that eat away the well-being of the people.

Chapter Four
Rebel without a Cause

21. Rebelliousness needs outlets

June 02, 2007

How should students treat their teachers?

This seems to be a no-brainer. Confucius said that we should respect our teachers as the ultimate authority. We can raise questions, but not question their authority. At the other extreme, we had periods of anti-Confucianism in the last century when teachers became a target of attack, even physical abuse.

A week ago, there was a replay of such an ugly moment. A 70-year-old teacher was conducting a geography class in a Beijing vocational school. About 20 teenagers were in class, some dozing off or mugging for a fellow student's video camera – and they were the nice ones.

A boy with an earring repeatedly taunted the teacher, using profanities like a drunken sailor, and snatching the teacher's baseball cap. Another boy threw an empty bottle at the teacher; and the whole class laughed in boisterous fun. The girl who made the video was so proud of their "achievement" she posted the clip online.

What is wrong with these youngsters? Don't they have a modicum of human decency?

To those with memories of the past, this episode is a painful reminder of what happened during the Cultural Revolution when students employed inventive means to humiliate and abuse their teachers, sometimes driving them to death. The kids in this recent incident explained they were just having some fun. They didn't mean any harm. Least of all did they expect the national outcry, which has scared some of them into hiding.

Surprisingly, I believe they were telling the truth.

Teenagers are naturally rebellious. Left on their own, some of them would do outrageous things they would regret when they mature. Contrary to conventional wisdom, kids are capable of cruelty.

When I was in high school, I witnessed a similar incident. It was winter and lots of snow had fallen outside the classroom. As soon as our math teacher turned around to write on the blackboard, snowballs would be thrown at him - not hitting him direct, but around him, so that there was a movie effect as if someone was dodging gunfire. One-third of the class joined in the action, the rest just laughed, and the teacher, like the one in the video, remained unfazed. Nobody thought how hurtful it was for him.

Mind you, this did not happen at the height of the chaotic Cultural Revolution, but after it ended. And it had nothing to do with the teaching quality. That teacher was one of the best in school. My classmates just thought he was weak and easy to pick on.

Apart from the inner devil in us that wanted to burst out, I can think of three reasons: boredom with what was being taught, uncertainty about the future, and not knowing how to have a meaningful conversation with a teacher.

There are ways to address these issues. Teaching materials and formats can be revised to add relevancy. More courses related to a student's job prospects and less pointless theorizing would help. But most of all, students should learn to rebel with respect.

Nowadays it is unrealistic for a teacher to shroud himself in an omniscient aura. The time of dispensing snippets of wisdom à la Confucius is gone forever. Today's students may have more sources of knowledge and, being adolescents, enjoy challenging authority figures whose mystique has been eroded by proximity. But they should know that to respect someone does not mean you have to agree with everything he says and to challenge him is not the same as debasing him.

Our culture tends to swing from one extreme to another on this matter. Students should respect teachers and other elders, and they should find rational outlets for their rebelliousness.

22. Youth facing dilemma of role models

May 27, 2006

China's youth is ripe for an underachiever as a role model, somebody like Bart Simpson.

You may think this sounds like a joke, but the competitive atmosphere that young people are thrust into nowadays has morphed into a boomerang, coming back with a vengeance. And not surprisingly, the top target is usually some kind of well-established authority figure.

Someone like Yu Qiuyu, for example.

Yu is a writer whose collections of essays contain a wealth of knowledge and insight, packaged in an elegant and mesmerizing style. To his peers, he is something of a rebel, giving up in the early 1990s the position of president of a Shanghai-based university and a fast-rising career of officialdom so that he could pursue a "purer" dream of writing. And that happened before he established himself as a best-selling author.

But to a Generation-X rebel like Han Han, Yu represents the "dreariness of middle-aged Chinese men". In a recent article, the young writer, who is also into car racing, expressed his "dislike for the way Yu looks and the way he does his hair, as if he uses some oily food as a towel". On top of it, Yu and his ilk "lack fun, honesty and imagination, and are too shrewd for their own good", and they "intoxicate

I don't agree with you.

themselves in self-devised grand concepts".

Obviously, this sentiment is echoed by quite a few people. When Yu Qiuyu "mispronounced" a word while judging a popular television contest early this month, thousands of fingers pointed at him. It turned out that Yu was not entirely wrong. The word in question could be pronounced in two ways. But for many young people, this is just an inconvenient technicality that should be ignored. Equally inconvenient is the fact that Yu is actually quite liberal when it comes to arts, education etc.

But since icons of erudition are only to be revered when they are dead, Yu should be attacked and hopefully toppled. If you browse online forums, you'll notice that netizens tend to lump together the real towering figures of wisdom with slick salesmen who are pitching their own agenda. If you say a word that goes against public sentiments, or more accurately the opinions of the younger generation, you are marked for vehement condemnation.

Nobody cares if your argument is well-thought-out and is infused with far-sightedness. It almost feels like a virtual replay of the Red Guards indiscriminately knocking down officials during the Cultural Revolution whether they were decent or corrupt.

However, it will be simplistic to generalize that young people are short on maturity or intelligence. Besides the habitual defiance of youth, an important factor is the pressure they face in eking out a livelihood given the cut-throat environment in education, job-hunting and housing. It is only too natural that they feel the older generation is hoarding all the opportunities.

This generational gap gives rise to a legion of angry young people who sometimes find an outlet for their frustration in targets that may be less intended than symbolized. For example, there are writers with a fraction of the talent of Yu Qiuyu but stash resources they have amassed over the decades. But they hardly raise eyebrows among the Gen-Xers.

Then there is the tradition of piety for authorities. The implied logic is, if you respect someone, you'll agree with his assessment on everything, especially in his sphere of specialty. Conversely, if you don't see eye to eye with an expert, you should regard him as a phony.

Sitting through a childhood of non-stop tests and made to worship idols of success mostly not of their own age group can be counterproductive. In a culture that believes in overachieving, heroes are bound to arise from a deliberate choice of underachievement.

Han Han's comments on Yu Qiuyu amounts to a Chinese version of "Eat my shorts", a Bart Simpson insult hurled at his school principal. He certainly has the right to his opinion. But he would have been more convincing if he had earned it.

What we sorely need is a culture of "respectfully disagreeing", ensuring that respecting and challenging authorities can coexist in the same person.

23. Don't let *gaokao* seal your fate

June 10, 2006

The annual ordeal for high-school graduates, known as the national college entrance examination (*gaokao*), was played out on a grand scale this past week. It is a ritual that dates back 1,500 years or so – a truly Chinese record that is in no danger of being topped by any other country.

It is supposed to be a level playing field where almost 10 million teenagers this year vie for what is basically a certificate of being better than half the population their age. The odds have been increasing in the past three decades. When I sat for it back in 1978, the enrolment ratio for my school was

maybe 1 in 50 or so. That should have made me feel like a smarty. But I didn't. Many of my classmates who, I was sure, were smarter failed or got into less sought-after schools. As a result, our roads diverged but, thanks to a spurt of entrepreneurship made possible by the reform policies, some of them came out ahead despite lacking "proper" credentials.

What I mean to say is, this system of selecting the brightest for the institution of "proud sons of heaven" is at best a loophole-ridden sieve that often fails to separate wheat from the chaff and at worst a smothering bag for real talent. It depends heavily on memorization of cut-and-dried snippets of textbook knowledge that most youngsters tend to gobble up without chewing and tasting. If anything, it is a fertile ground for conformity.

And if you've paid attention to reports of migrating exam-takers, you would know that the game is rigged in favor of big cities. Most colleges and universities – and the best – are located in metropolitan areas and enroll a disproportionate number of local students.

With the exception of the hinterland ethnic minorities, someone living in a poorer province has less chance of squeezing into the same school as someone from a richer one, given they score the same. In other words, kids in resource-deficient areas are not compensated for the state's inadequate investment in education, but are penalized for it.

It may sound paradoxical, but I'm not for abolishing the *gaokao* system. For all its quirks and partiality, it is one of the few mechanisms of meritocracy that we have.

And they are improving on it. For example, unconventional essays for the writing part of the language test no longer fall through cracks automatically. Some are even commended for originality. And now, even the topics are open-ended.

We can freely admit we hate *gaokao*, but do we have something better to replace it? What about a face-to-face interview, which should enable recruiters to gauge more accurately the potential of applicants, especially their EQs?

But sadly, it will also open a floodgate of corruption as impressions are more malleable than *gaokao* scores. Do you think that, given the same level of aptitude, someone with no social connections and no financial recourse will get the same treatment as someone whose parents can pull a few strings?

All the bad things you hear about *gaokao* are very true, and I can add some more to the list. But it's also a system that some brilliant kids from ordinary family background are able to break through.

Fortunately, there are now more channels for success than the "lone-plank bridge" of college education. Education can take a variety of forms, and being force-fed textbook golden rules are not necessarily the ideal for everyone. The world is full of people who fell off the plank and ended up in the sea of self-achievement.

Unfortunately, we still have this tradition of extolling *gaokao* scores and ranking people by the schools they are accepted into. Shouldn't we be eulogizing those who have made it big without going to the "brand-name schools", or even obtaining a college diploma? They are the ones who possess so much street smarts that they are then processed into theories by business school professors.

Complaints aside, I want to say to all the *gaokao* students: if you achieve a high score and get admitted into the school of your choice, my congratulations; but if you don't live up to your parents' expectation in a one-size-fits-all test, it doesn't mean you're a failure. There are so many things about you that *gaokao* cannot test, and you may well excel without participating in a flawed educational structure.

24. If it's honest work, what else matters?

December 02, 2006

Is it hypocritical to say one job is better than another?

I don't think so. An executive obviously earns more than a secretary. Even when a factory worker makes less than a farmer, the job – traditionally for urbanites – carries perks such as medical insurance and pension whereas a farmer is basically self-employed.

Then money is not everything, is it?

To see how jobs are ranked in our society, one needs only watch where college graduates swarm. For example, last year about a million of them applied for government jobs. In some cases, one had to edge out 1,000 competitors to get a position. That shows how "lofty" being a public servant is in the eyes of the nation's college students.

Gao Jian aims at the other end of the job spectrum when he openly sought a job as "a talking companion" (*peiliao*), an occupation somewhat like a counselor crossed with an au pair, but often appearing in the same sentence with hair salon girls and escorts. Adding further to the irony, Gao is fresh from the esteemed management program of Peking University, one of the nation's most prestigious mansions of higher learning.

A popular television host couldn't help taking a swipe at him for his monumental display of underachievement. Unexpectedly, Gao fought back. "I've been hunting for a job for the past six months, but no offer came. I'm helpless," he says in his blog. "Besides, to be a *peiliao* is to provide psychologi-

cal aid."

Gao admits he is not a straight-A student, but he passed all the courses and got the degree. Ma Bin, the CCTV2 host, quickly explained that it was not Gao's career goal he was picking apart, but his performance in school. One needs special training to be a counselor, added Ma, who hinted Gao was advertising the *peiliao* search as a gesture.

Whatever his intention, Gao Jian's attitude, as well as his action, is an antidote to the centuries-old practice of classifying people by their work environment. You may be a paper shuffler in a government office, and people will still kowtow to you; but if you operate a food stand on a street corner, even your children will feel humiliated. Gao was basically saying: "I'm from the most elitist school in China, but I cannot get a decent job, so I want to be a *peiliao*, maybe just for its shock or titillating value. So what?"

Our culture attaches prestige to positions that are closer to power centers and offer stable income. We discourage risk-taking endeavors such as entrepreneurship and innovation. The reason some of the nouveaux riches flaunt their wealth is to compensate for all the years of prejudice they suffered while they were still struggling as small-business owners.

When Lu Buxuan was found to be operating a butcher shop, the public was aghast: What a waste of talent! They heaved a collective sigh of disappointment. With the media avalanche, local authorities were compelled to employ the Peking University graduate as an archivist.

Then, another voice emerged from the public: What's so wrong with being a butcher? An educated person can make it more efficient and maybe turn it into a chain of supermarkets. So, instead of closing shop, he opened another one. Now Lu, the ultimate failure, has two butcher shops and a government job, straddling the world of free-market competition and coziness of government welfare. The last time the press checked on him, he had bought two apartments.

It is hard to disentangle what one does for a living from how much respect he or she commands. Even when people say: "I don't care what you do; everyone is equal," it has such an overtone of sanctimoniousness as if they were saying: "I know you're a pathetic loser, but I'll save your face by pretending a butcher is as highly regarded as a bureaucrat."

Only when a sizable middle class takes shape will people develop concepts such as the freedom to choose a career. Society should make sure that everyone has an equal chance to give play to his or her potential. But the career track selected by each individual should be based on the marriage of one's dreams and market needs.

Even then not everyone will respect another's choice of career. Those into writing novels or performing in the arts will probably be encouraged to get a day job while those who make millions a day from betting on the right stock will be ogled with envy.

That's the nature of this snobbish world. But at least more people – legions of happy rather than hapless Gao Jians – will snap back: "I like what I do. I don't break the law. I work for my money. And I don't care what you think about me."

25. In a hugging league of one's own

November 04, 2006

In recent weeks, small groups of young people appeared on downtown sidewalks in Changsha, Beijing and other cities, holding placards with the words "free hugs" and offered embraces to any passer-by who would care for one. Calling themselves "the hug league" (*bao bao tuan*), they said they were inspired by an international news story of a similar type and intended to promote human contact in the face of growing alienation in urban China.

Judging from media reports, the result has been less than warm and fuzzy. Onlookers were more often puzzled than exhilarated. Some saw them as "crazy". The "free huggers", if they can be so called, have inadvertently touched some cultural nerve. In my opinion, they are doing the right thing in the wrong way.

We Chinese, with the exception of some ethnic minorities, are not the touchy-feely type. Contrary to what is shown in our sentimental movies and television shows, we rarely run into each other's arms and cry our hearts out when the occasion calls for swelling background music.

We are raised in a culture of emotional restraint. We mark our meetings and departures with a wave of hand and a handshake of light touch. Not so long ago, even young lovers cuddling in public places were considered "imprudent".

But that does not mean we are immune to the wonderful feeling of human tactility. I remember my mother was visibly moved when I, in my adult years, held her hand for the first time while walking her across a busy street in the US. The circumstance made it more natural.

Think of it, even the handshake is a practice introduced from the West. The traditional Chinese greeting is to hold one's own hands. In the old days, physical contact between the sexes was strictly taboo. Doctors had to feel the pulse of female patients by means of a thread.

In a sense, the "free huggers" are blazing a trail by making the bear hug an acceptable form of human interaction in our society, free from sexual innuendos.

But cultures don't evolve overnight. Many women who opted to join chose those of the same gender. "It's hard to get rid of the old notion that man and woman should not have any physical contact," they explained. As one can see, the gist of the matter is to associate tactile sensations of this type with the warmth of human connection without creating unnecessary overtones of intimacy.

In the late 1970s when China was coming out of its self-spun cocoon, some feared that social dance would lead to sexual harassment. But the awkwardness was soon overcome as more and more people came to accept dancing with partners who were not their spouses as a perfectly normal form of recreation. Still, some people are more comfortable with partners of their own gender as one can witness in those dance-a-thons in public parks, which are often misunderstood by Western observers.

In China, it has no homosexual tinge at all for a teenager to walk hand in hand with, or hand on the shoulder of, a buddy of the same sex. But the overwhelming Western opinion is reshaping perceptions and more people realize that this is considered a public display of gay love and therefore begin to cringe from it.

In this environment of changing social mores and etiquette, how people act could be the working of many factors, including their personality. Some offer bear hugs to everyone they know while others would shiver at the prospect of medical personnel touching them with a stethoscope. The line between what is proper and improper often shifts with the sands of circumstances.

Offering hugs to strangers on the street is too radical a step to have any meaningful impact on our customs. If anything, the huggers should start with their loved ones.

26. Better teen body image with privacy

April 15, 2006

High school graduates in China live in constant anxiety. They have to sit through the fate-determining entrance exam, the result of which could more or less shape their future earning power and social status. But before that happens, they have to go through physical check-ups that require, for a brief moment, total nakedness. Many students tremble at the prospect. A few have reportedly used extreme means to dodge it.

The process described by some as "going through hell" takes place in a health facility. Typically, a dozen teenagers of the same gender will be grouped together, asked to disrobe and perform certain routines such as extending arms and legs and bending. The awkwardness is palpable, but most oblige after a few seconds of hesitation. Many choose to forget about the experience, and a few have written about it as "humiliating" or "shameful".

Obviously, the authorities were listening. There has been a spate of recent reports of hospitals changing policies on this part of the health exam. Some have extolled the termination of the "stripping" practice as a sign of regained respect for personal privacy.

Health facilities are indeed moving in the right direction. Teenagers are at an awkward age and tend to be thin-skinned about their bodies. Examination involving nudity should be handled with sensitivity and professionalism. It doesn't really add to the burden of administering thousands of testees on a single site. Cubicles with curtains can be erected without much cost, and those "touchy" tests could be done inside, away from the prying (more likely, equally uneasy) eyes of the milling crowd. Those who perform the test could explain what purpose it serves and why stripping is necessary. They could also prepare the students by telling them what exactly the procedure will involve before performing it. All this may help ease the nervousness of the youngsters.

But should nudity be called off simply because many are distressed by it? That doesn't preclude its necessity, which is up to medical professionals, not media commentators, to decide. If it's gratuitous,

sure, why keep it and ratchet up people's anguish? But what if it does indeed serve a health-related purpose?

I remember when I was in college, a schoolmate aroused suspicions because he never used the urinal while others were around and never went to the public bathroom, the only type available then. His roommates were curious about his real gender and wondered aloud whether he had the check-up. Of course, whether he was just hypersensitive or had a physical issue had little to do with others, and it didn't affect his academic performance either. But it seems to me that his doctor has a right to know and would be in a position to help him if there was a need.

China does not have a tradition of respecting individual privacy, so it is a welcome change that hospital authorities are showing awareness of the issue when handling routine check-up for high school students. On the other hand, China has a long tradition of body shame, which these reports have inadvertently reinforced.

There is no contradiction between respect for personal privacy and pride of one's own body. When Du Fu of Tang Dynasty wrote about his wife's "jade-like arms", some old scholars felt he stepped over the line. Shouldn't women in that era have covered all body parts except their faces?

Fortunately, we no longer live in a time when women were praised for cutting off their own arms when touched by male strangers. But that doesn't mean we have a healthy attitude toward body image. Self-loathing is rampant, especially among insecure teenagers. When one would think of jumping off a high building rather than go through the check-up process, it may be just as much a personal problem as improper hospital procedures.

Physical check-up is a strange place to bring up the topic of body perception. In western cultures, body image is often about young women trying to look like Barbie. Over here, there is the historical baggage that your body is something to be shameful of, especially the private parts. It is time we told our youngsters that, yes, they are private and people should not violate your privacy, but no, they are by no means loathsome.

Chapter Five
In the Wild World of the Web

27. Bloggers' revolution is largely overrated

December 23, 2006

Now that Time magazine has named "You" its Person of the Year, those addicted to the Internet have one more reason to tell their parents to beat it and leave them alone with their "revolution". You see, "you control the Information Age." It's "your world".

I really pity those who are computer illiterate but still want to exert some influence over their kids – kids who spend days and nights at Internet cafes, subsisting on instant noodles and dozing off in makeshift beds provided by the proprietor. Even though they have the gaze of zombies, their parents and teachers are on the receiving end of a mass campaign that marks them irrelevant – you might say a kinder and gentler version of the Cultural Revolution.

Don't get me wrong. I'm not denying the significance of Web 2.0 in particular or the Internet in general. There are many facets to the technology that are truly revolutionary. But the prediction that Web 2.0 will wipe out old media is overblown, and even sounds like the pomposity of the Red Guards.

Take YouTube for example. Much of the interesting stuff posted there is snippets from television shows, arguably part of the decaying old media. If you mention this content is copyrighted, you will be treated as if you are so old-fashioned you do not belong in this world. Revolutionaries do not need to worry about such trivialities as intellectual property rights, do they? IPR is for people with no imagination.

The technology essentially makes everyone a publisher, a broadcaster, a disseminator of news, views and entertainment. It will create new business models and reshape industries. But the old empires will simply crumble as the Red Guards said of the "capitalist roaders"? Give me a break!

In the US, the top 10 podcasts are all from media outlets like NPR and the New York Times. Why? Because they have been in the content business so long that they can consistently produce programs of the highest quality. Likewise, most of the decent blogs in this country are kept by professionals, especially those with experience in journalism. True, Wang Xiaofeng, cited by Time in its "You" cover story, cannot possibly publish his blogs in the magazine where he is a senior writer, but the quality of his writing is not something every blogger could attain just by getting a piece of online real estate and filling it with words.

To continue with the metaphor, everyone can get a virtual plot, but very few have the expertise to grow something of value on it. If you cared to wade through the millions of non-celebrity blogs, you would find that most read like a high-school student's diary and would not get more than a few dozen hits.

Imagine a newspaper where newsprint, printing costs and delivery are all free and every contribution from every reader is printed. It would probably come to 50,000 pages a day. Do you think this tome would be more valuable than Time magazine or the New York Times? Not to me. I would rather pay for a thinner version written and edited with the ethics, style and experience of a pro.

Of course, when an editor comes into play, some raw gems may slip through. That is the price we pay for subjective selection, in the same way that people in a democracy have representation in government rather than participate in every decision. It also leaves room for people whose talent may not fit traditional mass media but could flourish on the Web with its free-moving communities.

In a revolution, millions act out of zealotry and do not ask for anything in return, while one person or small group reaps huge benefit from it, all in the name of serving the public. The same applies to Web 2.0. Some websites used to pay a paltry fee for professional writers, now Sina "invites" you to be a blogger, meaning you can contribute to their advertising revenue by doing pro bono work. That does not bode well for people who write for a living.

It could be fun to roll around in the carnival of this revolution for a while. But ultimately one cannot survive on the ego boost of a few million non-paying clicks. The line might blur, but there will still be professionals and amateurs. Wikipedia may work because it functions as a non-profit organization. But if the whole sector is like this, it will largely fail as a "massive social experiment" because it disregards the law of economics and creates much more unfairness in the name of egalitarianism.

28. Let's stop lynching by public opinion

June 17, 2006

What is the difference between the masses and the mob?

For me, the former express their opinions rationally while the latter try to impose their judgment on others by means that are unacceptable in a civilized society.

Some outside China tend to see China's netizens in rosy colors – as mostly young, educated and well-informed. I bet they haven't surfed a typical Chinese Web forum. One is as likely to encounter fist-waving and vituperation as a sensible discussion, more so when it involves a hot topic. Something like the recent incident of a supposed adulterer hunted down by slogan-shouting throngs numbering in hundreds of thousands.

After a husband revealed online the details of his wife having an affair with a college student, thousands joined in the denunciation. Online sleuths later uncovered the true identity of the student, leading to calls of harassment and threats of various kinds, including "to chop off the heads of these adulterers, to pay for the sacrifice of the husband". Very pompous language reminiscent of the Cultural Revolution.

Did these people care whether or not the allegation was true? And if yes, did they have the right to act out their moral indignation in ways that were so obviously out of line with law and order?

Trial by virtual lynching has become the norm in China's cyberspace. When a controversy erupts, the rational voice is usually drowned out in vociferous condemnation.

I'm not saying our netizens are always wrong. As a matter of fact, they have a strong sense of justice – so strong that they see the world in only black and white. There's no room for shades of gray.

I don't like it even when their attacks hit the right target, for example, people who abuse animals or corrupt officials who try to cover up their actions. Justice by mob rule will not lead to more fairness and lawfulness. It will beget more twisted minds and more violence, virtual or real.

So, it doesn't matter whether or not the college student committed adultery. That is clearly a moral issue and the "moral court" of public opinion does not have the right to sentence him to expulsion from school or confinement to his house, let alone the harassing of his teachers and family members.

People need to know the line between expressing opinions and executing a legal verdict. The latter must be conducted with due process. While it is a good thing that ordinary people can participate in exposing the seamy sides of our society, over-enthusiasm may lead to witch-hunting. We are not entitled to be prosecutor, investigator, jury and judge all in one.

Some might blame all this on China's "lack of freedom of speech", but the irony is, the Internet generation has unprecedented access to information and education. They are the most attuned to Western lifestyles.

Yet, they – or more accurately many of them – exhibit characteristics commonly associated with the Red Guards. Worse yet, incidents like the hunting down of the adulterer were reportedly manipulated by Internet firms that need more eyeballs to make money. If that's true, it's truly the worst of both worlds – negative energy set in motion by commercial interests.

Online "flaming" wars exist everywhere, facilitated by anonymity. But in China they may have a self-propelling force that sweeps thousands, sometimes millions, into a frenzy. It is nearly impossible, even for the most respected scholars, to give voice to dissension.

Thinking of it, this does have something to do with our culture. For thousands of years, we have not really cultivated enough space for different voices. They are cast away as "wrong" and often ostracized. We need to realize that, even if obviously wrong, as long as they make good arguments, they serve the purpose of contributing to a well-balanced society. Harmony does not necessitate we speak as one.

Maybe the Web mob is a vociferous minority. Sometimes, I doubt it. But it can ruin the prospects of rational discourse. I'm not suggesting it be silenced – it should not. But it should be made aware that there is a sensible alternative to expressing oneself using a mouse and keyboard to stage a public lynching.

29. Cat killers could be given alternatives

March 11, 2006

"Cats" is now being played out in China.

No, not the Andrew Lloyd Webber musical, but a real-life horror starring live kittens, equally cute bimbos, kinky high-heels and cruelty so disgusting that even the nation's angry young men find nothing to cheer about.

Recent media reports have uncovered a smattering of websites that offer photos and video segments showing fashionable women cuddling kitties and then stomping them to death with their stiletto heels.

We're not talking about a few sick people venting out anger on their pets. It's an underground business with sexy ladies doing the jobs of killers for profit. The mind-blowing thing is, there are people who actually pay real money to access these images.

The outcry is thunderous enough to drown out any rationale. Yes, these people are disturbed individuals, but what can we do about them and their behavior?

Well, the first solution is the "legal weapon". Many cite laws from West-

ern nations that protect animal rights and call for similar laws to be passed in China. This may work to wipe out commercial cat-killing videos, but may mean little to those who engage in such acts in the privacy of their own homes. Our law enforcement officers are straining their resources to solve murder mysteries where victims are human, and it's unlikely the same efforts could be applied to felines.

If we're going to use a law for the main purpose of deterrence, why not let the moral court do the job? As we have seen, public opinion can make would-be cat killers, however gorgeous they are, look like the proverbial mice trying to cross a busy street.

Then there's the question of why people enjoy these images. It may come as a shock to many in China, but sadism is nothing new. It exists everywhere in the world, in the hidden parts of every person.

Rational as we are, most of us can suppress these feelings because we're fully aware that, by emitting them, we will be harming others. The underpinning of a civilization says one should not, in the process of seeking self-satisfaction, destroy lives and happiness of others.

However, sadism is a psychological disorder that cannot be regulated out of existence. Sadists have to find an outlet. Sadistic urges can often be channeled to bloody sports. Most of the war movies and computer games also function as safe outlets for potential killing machines. The pleasure derived from these alternative activities may not always be sexual in nature. Those with a penchant for violence and brutality may not know why they feel that way and don't always know how to manage it. This is where professional help comes in.

In the online world of anonymity, many people have freely admitted that they actually enjoyed the cat-squashing pictures. That may make us look like a world of perverts, but it's better than suppressing the glee and pretending it exists only among a few sickos.

Having recognized the problem, we can tackle it in a rational way. We should help those with sadistic inclinations to seek counseling. And, at the very least, we can install a punching bag in the shape of a kitten for them to let off steam.

30. Starbucks in the Forbidden City

January 20, 2007

Yang Zaibao was a screen icon of heroism and virility in the early 1980s. His image was used to hawk some male enhancement products without his approval. When he sued the offending company, the media condemned it for damaging Yang's good name, but hardly anyone mentioned the illegal use of copyrighted material. In the eyes of the public, the culprit was the less than honorable nature of the advertisement. By extension, if it had been a sound product such as a calendar, people would probably not have raised an eyebrow.

No need to hide, you foreign devil!

Fast-forward 25 years. Half a million Chinese netizens are fuming over the presence of Starbucks in the Forbidden City. They are protesting the cultural clash while they should detest the rampant commercialism.

It is quite common for those with strong emotions to develop tunnel vision and overlook the big picture. The critical factor in both of the above cases is legality. The law has clearly stipulated that commercializing a person's image without his consent is illegal, and which advertiser did the plagiarizing was irrelevant. Likewise, if laws and regulations permit restaurateurs to operate in the former imperial palace, then the Seattle-headquartered coffee shop

did nothing wrong.

If citizens feel this is a big mistake, they should push to revise the law in the first place.

As a matter of fact, much of the disapproval is targeted at a very subjective realm of ethics and aesthetics. The product for which Yang's photo was plastered around is probably no longer considered ignominious. As for the coffee outlet, it is just as murky as to what is right or wrong.

Personally, I think the Starbucks shop blends in quite well with the environment. If it had been a giant golden arch, I would have strongly objected.

I guess it is the foreignness of the vendor that critics are pointing fingers at. In that case, they should propose to forbid all foreign retailers from, say, world heritage sites. But then, what if some Chinese company bought a majority stake in Starbucks? Would that make it more palatable for a quintessentially Chinese locale as the Forbidden City? In the age of globalization, this scenario is not implausible.

OK, if it's not the ownership that's worrying them, we can shift to the cultural aspect. In many historic downtowns of European and American cities, there are Chinese restaurants. Do they mar the integrity of the sites? On the contrary, local tourism brochures tout them as a display of multicultural color.

I surmise it is the purity of the site that people want to safeguard. But purity is relative. When we look at a historic building, it usually boasts additions and reconstructions that reflect later eras. Yes, some of the changes are deplorable, but others are accepted. Likewise, a Starbucks in the old palace could be construed as an interesting fusion of old and new and a sign of progress as well as an intrusion.

Of course, public opinion should be taken seriously. The opening of the outlet should have been preceded by consultation with heritage protection experts and, if necessary, by public hearings. More importantly, rampant commercialization must be curtailed in such locations, which is far more urgent than moving out one Starbucks store.

If you travel around the country, you'll see lots of structures that are literally blots on the landscape. The builders often have connections with local officials. And it is money and power, without the restraints of rules, public opinion or aesthetic considerations, that drive such projects.

The online horde is well intentioned but misguided. They are trying to root out one small evil – at least what they consider to be evil – while leaving out the real evil.

Note: Starbucks vacated from the Forbidden City in July, 2007.

31. Mr. Mayor, a netizen is calling

August 11, 2007

The Internet is a mind-boggling platform when it comes to communication. Perfect strangers can meet there and conduct meaningful conversations, which may lead to special relationships and, in some cases, even marriage.

This week, a 32-year-old Chongqing resident sent an e-mail to the Party secretary of the municipality, and soon got a response from the leading official of this province-level administration. One more exchange later, he was summoned to a face-to-face meeting with both the secretary and the mayor.

This was widely reported by the press and dissected from every angle by pundits. But what does it really mean?

Du Shulin, the netizen, had submitted a 10-point proposal on how to build up his hometown - this vast municipality that incorporates a downtown metropolis and large swathe of countryside. He did it in answer to Party Secretary Wang Yang's call for good ideas.

What made it special, it seems, was that Wang took the trouble to respond and then meet him for further dialogue; and what made it newsworthy was the identity of this "ordinary citizen" – a netizen nonetheless.

This cannot hold water, though. If he had sent in his proposal via telephone or post, this would probably be buried in the local paper and never picked up by others. And what's so special about being a netizen?

Suffice it to say, China's online population is a skewed reflection of the general public. But as it grows to 162 million strong, it is losing more and more of its uniqueness as a demographic. In other words, this would not have moved more quills of appreciation than necessary if the official already had regular channels of communication with his citizenry.

However, we must remember that the Internet has taken on an irreplaceable role when it comes to

mass rejection of unpopular policies. When Xiamen planned to build a facility of potential chemical hazard in close proximity to residential districts, it was the Internet that allowed citizens to aggregate their voices and ultimately block the project from turning into a local nightmare.

In my understanding, the Internet is just icing on the cake for regular government-citizen communication. If an official picks the brains of only a select group, e-mail suggestions are not going to pile up on his desk. But if he makes an extreme move that offends a significant portion of the populace, the Internet – and to some extent, mobile short messaging – can give voice to the public that otherwise cannot be heard.

The Chongqing official deserves plaudits for his willingness for citizen brainstorming. While it is unrealistic for an official of his stature to sit down and talk to everyone who sends in advice, a public official should have a mechanism to hear out public opinion.

Letters and e-mails should be sorted and forwarded to the right departments. They should be categorized: those that require immediate action should be effectively addressed, and those that cannot be solved should be explained to the sender. Issues of mass interest should be publicized in the media to raise awareness.

There is an undertone to the national media's hyping of the Chongqing story: People extol what that official did because it was extraordinary. He went out of his way to welcome public opinion. If most officials were open to such grassroots input, the story would not have much news value.

So, it is important to turn an exception, more or less, into a norm. Yes, some officials know how to reach out and talk to their constituents, but others should see them as role models and make an effort to improve discourse with those they serve. Social harmony is only possible when public has a say in the decision-making at city hall.

32. Netizen's arguments do not sit well with real life people

August 12, 2006

Offering your bus seat to someone in need (*rang zuo*) seems to be the right thing to do regardless of geography, culture or economic status. A recent backlash proves that not everyone takes it as such.

Earlier this year, Zhengzhou in central China installed an incentive scheme for *rang zuo*. That set off an online debate. "Why should I give my seat to an elderly person? It's the young who need it more because they take off in the early morning while not fully awake and drag themselves home after a day of exhausting work," wrote one blogger. The author further noted that senior citizens already enjoy benefits such as free rides. This treatment should be suspended during the rush hours to relieve bus congestion, he suggested.

I thought I was blasé about outrageous opinions in the cyberspace, but this really jolted me. What's more frightening is that the author enjoyed wide support from about 60 percent of the online population who participated in the debate on who's more worthy of a bus seat, according to one analyst.

What is wrong with these people? Aren't they going to get old someday and what will they think when a youth sitting in a bus seat turns a blind eye to them standing nearby? Obviously it is too early for them to conjure up this scenario.

Most buses in Chinese cities are plastered with signs that read: "Please *rang zuo* to the elderly, the handicapped, the pregnant and women with young children." There are usually a few seats marked for this purpose.

The online outpouring of dissension is perplexing because it contradicts what I've observed in the real world of human interaction. In Beijing and Guangzhou, where I take the bus frequently, I've rarely seen a case of the four types of "needy" passengers getting the cold treatment.

On the contrary, when a person who looks older than 60 steps in, someone nearby will immediate vacate his or her seat. Occasionally the ticket seller will yell: "Who will *rang zuo* to this grandma?"

It is part of the social etiquette. People do it as if by intuition. There is no whiff of "doing something good so that I can write about it for my school assignment," which was sometimes apparent in the 1980s. Well, every kid in China is supposed to do essays on a "meaningful small thing".

It is a small gesture of altruism at the expense of a little discomfort to oneself.

I don't like the way that some teachers instill the notion in youngsters that it is some kind of moral grandstanding. It just seems to be natural. (By the way, we do not have the lady-first tradition of *rang zuo* to young women. That would imply they are weaker.)

But to quibble about who is more in need of a seat just seems misguided. It is not a sign of being rational, but rather, of being mean. Sure, there are young people who may need the seat more than an elderly person, and I don't think anybody is legally or morally obligated to *rang zuo*. But if there's not a single person on a whole bus who would perform this random act of kindness, there would be something upsettingly wrong with our society.

But what shall I make out of the online opinion? I have often been warned not to interpret online voices as representative of the real world. If I talk to people on the street or even in the hinterland, I would get mostly balanced feedback that reflects common sense. But if I sample the netizens, it's usually the most virulent that stands out.

Sometimes I even doubt whether they accurately reflect the online demographic, which tends to be young and educated. Some from this group once told me that they had to be very opinionated in order to be heard and noticed in the vociferous cyberworld. Wang Xiaofeng, a renowned blogger, does not hide his contempt for this group. He thinks they are just extremely selfish.

It would be interesting if some pollster would conduct an in-depth survey about the attitude of the young, say, those born after 1980. Just start with *rang zuo*. I still believe that most would not hesitate to offer their bus seats to people commonly believed to be more in need of them.

What if the result comes out more in tandem with the online majority? I dare not think about it. It sends shivers down my spine.

Chapter Six
Moral Vortex

33. When a pop star went gay bashing

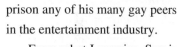

August 18, 2007

When an entertainment celebrity takes a moral stand, it often goes beyond personal belief. That is why the moral crusade of a Chinese television star has turned into an eye-catching headline.

Sun Haiying, who achieved stardom with a popular drama series, told a reporter that homosexuality is "criminal in nature". That certainly goes against both common sense and the legal definition, because China long ago decriminalized the behavior. So there is little danger that Sun will send to prison any of his many gay peers in the entertainment industry.

From what I surmise, Sun is not threatening prosecution for gays. The Chinese word "*zui*", which he used in the interview, could be construed in either a legal sense or a religious context. The English translation for the latter is "sin", and unsurprisingly many among the conservative right in the West would agree with Sun on his judgment of gays and lesbians.

While I respect Sun for upholding his opinion, I lament that he made a private conviction into a public controversy. Celebrities have much more clout than ordinary citizens. When they take a stance for or against an issue, it is bound to have repercussions.

When Angelina Jolie adopts foreign orphans, her high-profile acts are a call to attention to either the misery of the unfortunate or to her self-righteous image. When Chinese actor Pu Cunxin appears in ads for protecting the rights of AIDS patients, he is doing much more than a simple financial donation. In both cases, stars threw their weight around and tried to influence others.

Historically, Chinese people have been very tolerant towards homosexuality. From online polls, one gets the impression that the majority would respect others' lifestyle. Sun's repugnance could be deeply moral or religious, in which case the dominant argument is, if homosexuality spreads like a wildfire, the human race would ultimately be extinct.

That is a fallacy. Homosexuality will never replace heterosexuality as the majority sexual orientation. It is congenital but not contagious. The reason he may feel otherwise is more gays are willing to come out of the closet nowadays and some adopt an in-your-face strategy, thrusting their presence into mainstream consciousness in an effort to fight discrimination.

From a practical point of view, with tens of millions more men than women in the country, gays can rectify the gender imbalance in their small way. Some people may laugh at the notion, but at least one Chinese scholar is actually serious about it as a solution.

There is also a chance that Sun Haiying derived his bigotry from empirical experience. He may be abhorred by the gays he knows. Herein lies the danger of equating a few unscientific samples with the whole demographic.

By coincidence, this week's other "weird" story showed the flip side of Sun's homophobia. Hengyuanxiang, a Shanghai-based fabric maker, broadcast its recruitment of lefties for middle-management positions. The reason? They tend to be smart.

As a matter of fact, a parallel can be drawn between gays and lefties: Both are minorities with less than 10 percent of the population; both are widely considered congenital but are often put through special "correction treatment" while young; both come with certain stereotypes, either flattering or derogatory.

People like Sun Haiying may not realize that a group with tens of millions of people cannot be neatly categorized with one pithy adjective, complimentary or pejorative. This would be like fortune-telling that boils down all the people born on the same day or in the same month to one personality and one fate.

Simplification could be fun in trivial things such as horoscopes, but it leads to prejudice when applied with moral standards.

34. Suicide as a spectacle

January 06, 2007

The New Year bells had hardly stopped tolling, when something outwardly tragicomic but inherently disturbing happened in Chengdu, Sichuan.

On Tuesday morning, a young woman was contemplating jumping off a six-story building. It took the police and firefighters five hours to talk the emotional distressed out of it and move her to safety.

But that made some people very unhappy – some onlookers who had gathered on the street to witness the crisis. According to press reports, many of them "held out their necks as if they were ducks dangling from someone's hands."

The mood was boisterously festive. Some yelled: "Come on! Jump!" Others took out their cellphones and snapped pictures or called their friends, asking them to "come and enjoy the spectacle". Still others were so impatient that they complained: "She's just pretending. Why didn't she jump before the police arrived?"

A young man joined in and effectively played the male lead of the revelry by sitting on the window of an opposite building and

playing a guitar.

Everyone booed in disappointment when the woman was rescued.

One thing these people said was right. The woman did not want to kill herself. Most suicide attempts are cries for help or attention. Migrant workers who threaten to jump off high-rise buildings do it just to get the wages owed to them. People jilted in love usually go through a difficult time of loss and reconciliation. They are not determined to die, but are vulnerable nonetheless.

It was, therefore, terrible for the crowd to act the way they did. Are their lives so pathetically uneventful that they had to witness a possible suicide for pleasure? Wouldn't they feel guilty if she had really jumped? What if she were someone they knew – a friend, a family member or simply an acquaintance? I wouldn't say these people were bloodthirsty, but their minds were somewhat twisted. Worse yet, their behavior did suggest something bigger, something about us as a people who have broken out of moral shackles of one kind but have yet to find a new code of ethics.

The incident inevitably reminds one of an episode in one of Lu Xun's stories: A young man was being executed for his involvement in revolutionary activities. A big crowd looked on with nothing but indifference and curiosity on their faces.

The great Chinese writer got inspiration from newsreels he saw when he was a medical student in Japan. He was ashamed that his own compatriots could be so insensitive. That gave him a jolt that the Chinese people needed a writer who would shake them out of their stupor more than a physician who would heal them of bodily wounds.

Most people have attributed this apathy to dire poverty and lack of education. Obviously, this analysis no longer applies. The throng in Chengdu was most likely well fed and adequately educated. Besides their curiosity, the state of mind was different from the spectators at the execution some 100 years ago.

For a long time we were deprived of all good clean fun. Once the floodgates opened, everything rushed out, including the basest instincts. This is entertainment with a vengeance, what popular websites call "entertaining to death". People – hopefully a minority – do not seem to know when to laugh and when to cry, or at the very minimum, to keep a straight face and be appropriately solemn. They have mistaken human decency for hypocrisy.

Why does a society that shapes a budding mind with awe and reverence end up with adults who fail to respect anything, even life itself? Could it be that such qualities as helping the weak and unfortunate are instilled rather than inbred and become slogans to be recited rather than virtues to be integrated?

This is not a cultural issue. Both Chinese and Western cultures teach one to be kind and helpful. However, we are living in a time of such fast change that we can almost feel the sands shifting under our feet. Reattaching what was cut off by political turmoil might be futile, but the garden of moral principles will certainly grow and bloom again. It will take time because the weeds of warped minds can only be corrected by enlightenment.

35. Advocating condom use does not equal legalizing prostitution

September 16, 2006

On September 6, newspapers in Chongqing carried this item on a local government proclamation: All sex-related entertainment venues must provide condoms. The goal is to be achieved in five years, through the joint efforts of health, commerce and public security departments in five of the districts and counties of this sprawling municipality in Southwest China.

Local authorities may have hoped that only those who needed to know would notice it, but pundits swooped in from across China. Their denunciations have been loud and clear. Doesn't the decree imply that prostitution is legal in this town? They cry.

I asked a similar question 20 years ago while living in San Francisco. At the height of the AIDS epidemic, the city government introduced a policy that allowed drug users to obtain clean needles, free of charge.

Why should taxpayers foot the bill for these addicts' habits? Besides, won't it encourage drug addiction? And isn't drug use supposed to be illegal anyway?

But I wasn't as wise then as I am now. Basically I was looking at the issue through a moral prism, not taking into account that the kaleidoscopic happenings in the real world cannot be neatly categorized in black-and-white terms. It is true that prostitution is illegal in China as in most other countries. The question is, could the practice be outlawed out of existence?

There are millions of entertainment venues – karaoke bars, massage parlors, hair salons that may or may not venture into the shady territory. They're not supposed to, but there is a reason, or rather multiple reasons, that some take the risk to offer different sex services. Top on the list of reasons is demand.

And you can't blame the police for not trying to stop it. They have tried all kinds of ways – some ethical and others less so. It is not unknown for corrupt cops to collude with hookers to blackmail their Johns. But none of the police's anti-prostitution drives have put a visible dent in the business.

The only way to ensure prostitution is wiped off the surface of this land would be to keep human movement to an absolute minimum, or simply install a police state. If history is any indication, neither of these options is attractive.

Unless one insists on the total extermination approach, one has to consider the existence of vice as part of our social fabric. One has to use logic to analyze the whole process and find the feasible solution.

For example, the old way was to catch prostitutes "red-handed", meaning with condoms in their pockets or in their drawers. So, how do you think they would react? They would forego the incriminating evidence by simply not using them.

Now, China is on the cusp of an AIDS crisis, with the virus threatening to spread to the general population from more concentrated groups such as drug addicts and prostitutes. Discouraging the latter from using condoms would add fuel to a simmering flame, making it easier for the blaze to engulf us all.

As for the accusation that Chongqing is trying to legalize prostitution, I don't know whether, in China, a municipal government has the right to do that. I believe this is reading too much into the policy. Tolerating something is not the same as advocating it. Unfortunately many people blur the line, either deliberately or out of habit.

There are many things in our society that should not exist. Jaywalking and spitting in public come into mind. Many cities have rules that slap these offenders with a financial penalty. But they are enforced haphazardly at best. Why? It is simply not possible to enforce every misdemeanor of this kind. Just imagine how many cops we would need to deploy to catch every jaywalker or spitter.

Moral purists are constantly striving for a perfect world, but the world we live in is far from perfect. If we formulate our rules and regulations based on their lofty ideals rather than reality, we'll hurtle down to hell on a road paved with good intentions.

Critics may have taken the moral high ground, but it is the Chongqing authorities who are acting out of a sense of responsibility.

36. Soothed feet, clean conscience

April 12, 2008

In 1995, the Reichstag building in Berlin was wrapped in white sheets by the artists Christo and Jeanne-Claude as an art project.

Recently, a building in the city of Zhangjiajie, Hunan Province, seemed to be wrapped in red sheets. The intention was not to be artistic, though, as the vertical banners all bore congratulatory messages from an array of government agencies, including the tax bureau, the court and the procurator's office – all for the celebration of a foot-washing business.

When photos of the banner-covered building surfaced online, they drew a barrage of condemnation: How could local authorities join hands with unsavory elements in such a blatant display of solidarity? Are they supposed to be the cat and the mouse?

Without digging deeper, and in the absence of incriminating evidence, this is reading too much into the photos. The banners are, in essence, alternatives for the more common baskets of flowers that friends, peers and even rivals send on such occasions.

Part of the controversy lies in the nature of the business of foot washing, or rather, foot massaging. Like similar services, such as saunas, hair salons and massage parlors, it is often lumped with the world's oldest trade, or, serves as a front for that business, which is illegal in China.

Assuming innocence before proving otherwise, we should refrain from jumping to the conclusion that this particular venue, which has just opened its doors, is guilty by association. Foot massaging, which may sound quaint to some, sprouted in China in the late 1990s and employed a huge army of young and barely skilled migrants. Many cities see the industry as delivery from poverty and even a gateway into prosperity. The trickle-down effect is palpable as the business is labor intensive, but resource light.

If anything, foot massaging is less likely to morph into contact of the intimate kind than regular massaging because it involves only the body parts below the knees and is performed in the presence of

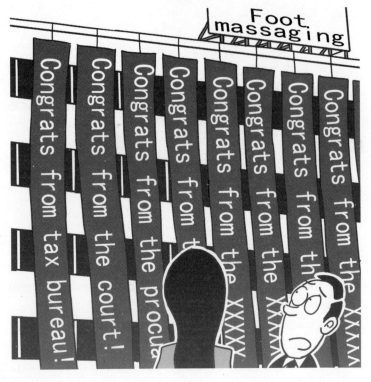

other patrons, sometimes in big halls.

It so happens that I had a foot-massaging adventure in Zhangjiajie, which is where the latest brouhaha took place. After two days of trekking in the nearby scenic mountains, a group of us were guided – or goaded – to a place for a "free foot massage".

As soon as we made ourselves comfortable in a room arranged like a meeting hall, two dozen young men and women emerged, each holding a basin of water. They wore big smiles, and without hesitation, rolled up our pants and started rubbing.

Just as some of us were dozing off, a sharp-looking middle-aged man in a fancy suit jumped onto a small podium. He started to enumerate the countless benefits of some herbal medicine, or rather, diet supplement. God, he was eloquent! But nobody budged. We all wanted the freebie without the over-priced placebo.

Finally, someone said: "I'll buy one. I don't think we'll be let go without shelling out a single yuan."

Shouldn't local authorities, especially law enforcement, ensure such businesses avoid creeping into shady territory? Of course. They should not become the umbrella to shelter local businesses from anything unethical or illegal. That is the bottom line. But on the other hand, there is nothing wrong with maintaining a buddy-buddy relationship with those they tax and protect, and most of all, serve.

Am I so naive as to be blind to the obvious white-way, black-way (read: cop and mafia) conspiracy? For me, a string of banners does not constitute even circumstantial evidence.

37. History textbook in soft focus

September 09, 2006

Revising a history textbook is a dangerous thing. People who are used to the old version will feel cheated and find a thousand faults. People who start with the new may doubt your motives and suspect they are not getting a balanced account.

The new history textbook adopted in Shanghai has ruffled a lot of feathers, for different reasons. The biggest reason mentioned in Chinese media is actually the most trivial: No netspeak is allowed. Since when do textbooks accommodate words such as MM (beautiful girl), dragon (ugly girl) or PK (player killer)?

I've always advocated more freedom for usage of slang, but a formal textbook is not the right platform for such expressiveness because it is not a personalized and entertaining narration like the one delivered by Professor Yi Zhongtian to a massive television audience. But that's a topic for another column.

The significance of the new Shanghai textbook lies not in its resistance towards words in vogue, but in its fundamentally revolutionary approach to history. And personally, I believe it is the right approach.

It has toned down descriptions of peasant uprisings and violent dynastic changes. In their place is more content about innovation and culture. It would be tempting to interpret it as an answer to the call for "a harmonious society". But such politicizing, though not wrong, may be a little shallow.

The learning of history in a Chinese classroom had always been made up of memorizing lengthy dynastic lineages, with their numerous names and dates. There is no room for interpretation: you are supposed to see it only from the one perspective sanctified by the textbook.

And honestly, the old approach is not balanced. It places too much emphasis on destructive events and their dynamics, often leaving them out of historical context. One gets the sense that if you belong to the ruling class, your job is to oppress the people; and if you are a *laobaixing* (hoi polloi), you

should automatically hate the landlords and the powers-that-be and overthrow them at the first chance you get.

No wonder youngsters nowadays cheer online whenever news of the killing of a billionaire or an official emerges. If you sow hatred, you reap hatred.

That is especially true for teenagers, who are not mature enough to receive a comprehensive and nuanced chronicling of historic events. Actually, in our society, even some adults have difficulty digesting the complexities of history because we, in our formative years, had been fed a black-and-white, cut-and-dried rendition.

I'm not suggesting we should omit wars and revolutions all together. But given the limited time for history teaching in our packed high-school curriculum, the shift of focus to positive things in history – the creations that have enriched us, the civilizations that have made us who we are – is an encouraging one.

Is it going from one extreme to another? Not necessarily. For one thing, this approach will make a more wholesome person out of the high-school student. This is not the same as blanket whitewashing if you encourage the teenager to dig deeper into history while in college and come up with more sophisticated interpretations.

Suppose the student does not go to college or pore over those thick tomes. It is still better, I'm convinced, that he or she remains blissfully ignorant than blindly hating everyone who is richer or who occupies a higher position.

Speaking of condensations and omissions, there are recent events, like the Great Leap Forward and the Cultural Revolution, that have shaped whole generations but are squeezed to only a brief mention, in both the old and new editions. It is lamentable, but for high-schoolers, it is probably necessary.

A proper education should include learning about one's own national history and also world history. That does not mean only the happenings that we would love to hear. There is plenty of ugliness in our history that we should know and understand. As they say, those who forget history are doomed to repeat it.

Reversing the sequence of teaching may sound innocuous, but can lead to the breeding of warped minds, with severe inferiority or superiority complexes and irrational distrust of fellow human beings.

The Shanghai textbook is a step in the right direction. And from the attacks from those who cling to the outdated way of thinking, it may prove to be a significant one.

38. Where are our older workers?

| October 28, 2006 |

Last week, I experienced what can best be described as a "blessing in disguise" or "sweet misfortune". I was struck down by a bout of flu and had to get intravenous shots. The hospital I visited was staffed by people who were so young and good-looking that they could have been the cast of a soap opera - the kind with multiple pairs of young lovers. Not even *E.R.* could hold a candle to it.

"Where are the middle-aged nurses?" I wondered. "Surely, there are 'old experts' who are not fashion magazine cover material." But they were nowhere in sight. Bored, I picked up a newspaper. A line-up of mug shots caught my attention. They featured similar faces of the movie starlet types. "Why do they put beauty contestants in the news section?" I asked myself.

It turned out that these were not models or singers, but teachers vying for the title of "Charming Teacher" in the city of Xuzhou, Jiangsu Province. As reported, the contest was patterned after the famous *Supergirls*.

Now, I am not so old-school as

to suggest that teachers look dour, forbidding and grim. On the contrary, I feel teachers should refrain from talking down to students and treat them as friends. In terms of appearance, if they want to make themselves pretty, it is their right – as long as the look is not too avant-garde.

But looks or no looks, this is not essential to what makes up a good teacher, which is how most people interpret the "Charming Teacher" title. A teacher's "charm" lies first and foremost in the way he or she teaches.

Of course, I cannot dispute that those who made the list were good teachers with good looks to boot. As a matter of fact, I doubt anyone can evaluate teachers based on some online information, especially photographs. Even if I were a student of one of them, I could pass judgment on that person alone. Only a panel of judges who sit in classes of all of them can make comparisons. Judging from the results, I think they have selected beautiful people who happen to be teachers. Otherwise, how can one justify that there are no middle-aged or old teachers in the league?

The youth culture, often called "the beauty economy" in China, is surging with a vengeance. A generation ago, even fashion models were frowned upon; but now, half-naked bodies are being used to hawk almost any merchandise. As a form of entertainment there is nothing wrong with it as people are naturally drawn to youth and beauty and it is something to flaunt if you've got it. So, it is okay if the teachers' contest is just another name for a beauty pageant.

But there are many areas where beauty simply does not play a decisive role, or any role at all. When you launch a rocket, do you want a scientist who looks like a movie star or someone who can get the job done? You may point out that there is actually no contradiction between the two qualifications: One can be both good-looking and competent. That is right. But, most news items with "beautiful women" in the title are titillations with no substance.

Take the recent story of a town in Chongqing that plans to recreate "a women's kingdom", a matriarchal society. The idea that men "float" around from family to family – à la the Mosuo people in Yunnan Province – is just too tempting for some. But wake up! This is only a theme park and everything in it is a show.

Like many creative ideas, this one got a head start by conjuring up "beautiful women in provocative situations". It is a game that people, including us in the media, play to grab attention. And it is up to each individual to see through the smoke and mirror of a gorgeous facade to determine whether there is truly something inside.

Back at the hospital of beau monde, after two days of flu shots, my fever did not come down – it rose even higher. Maybe the whole thing was a coincidence. Maybe they were indeed actors who gave me placebos after all.

39. Tiger, tiger! Faking bright

Before the smoke and dust surrounding the South China tiger photos taken in Shaanxi Province settled, someone claimed to have successfully photographed the big cat – widely believed to be extinct in China – in Hunan province. This time, unlike the still images from Shaanxi, it was a 20-second video clip with a very mobile animal.

Shortly afterwards, the local authorities, after an investigation, revealed that the whole thing was a hoax. It turned out that a television reporter had conspired with a circus manager to execute the better-than-Shaanxi idea. The circus has a Northeastern tiger. The two moved it to a patch of woods where they shot the clip. You have to admit that it was a giant leap up in the echelon of make-believe from the previous poster blowup – at least that's what most people believe it to be.

And unlike the Shaanxi authorities whose investigations are still on, the Hunan leaders were decisive. Yes, it was a fake even though this one involved a genuine tiger.

But there are similarities as well. In both cases, some local experts were quick to confirm the authenticity of the tiger!

The most brilliant bon mot came up during the investigation. A developer of local tourism who was found to have masterminded the ruse, nonchalantly justified the hoax. He told reporters that tourism is all about make-believe. "Now that you guys have killed the tiger concept, we'll have to create new ones, maybe the South China leopard."

He went on to argue that the local county is mountainous, unfit for farming. Tourism is a way out of poverty. County officials have designated it as a strategy to "feed and enliven" the people. "Tourism needs capital. But it needs creativity even more. The tiger could have been a spark."

Before I could laugh him off as insane, I walked down the memory lane to think of all the places I had visited. In one place near an old town in Yunnan, I – and a group of tourism scholars – were led to a mountainside with many totem poles that looked like 3,000 years old. We were told of the ancient civilizations that once flourished there.

Honestly, we were impressed. The whole place had some primitive power and beauty. Then, I turned to the Australian professor in our group: "Forgive my ignorance, but I've never heard of this place. It looks at least as impressive as Stonehenge."

"Well, I have to be honest, too. I haven't heard of it either, and I'm supposed to be an expert on this area," he whispered to me.

Our eyes were locked in a moment of epiphany as we burst out in one voice: "This is a theme park!"

There is nothing wrong with building a theme park that resembles a prehistoric monument, imaginary or real. But you have to inform the public.

On the contrary, the public has to play the sleuth. Another incident I remember involved a consumer who bought a terra-cotta soldier in a Beijing department store, priced 8,000 yuan. She sued the store when she found it was just an imitation. The store owner retorted: "Of course it's fake. Would a real one sell for only thousands? It would be priceless and it's against the law to trade relics of such importance."

The trouble could have easily been avoided if the item included "imitation" in its description.

I cannot but admire those who went to such lengths to get their hometowns into hot destinations of tourism. With this kind of imagination, they could have come up with ideas that hook both reporters and tourists – ideas not grounded in reality but built in castles in the air. People go and visit places of historic significance, but they may also like to be taken sometimes on rides of pure fantasy.

Chapter Seven
Sex, Lies and Marriage

40. Metrosexuals on the rise

August 07, 2006

It's official: China has entered the age of the metrosexual.

(Members of the international press, just a reminder: This is a personal column, not a disguised version of a government proclamation.)

Last year, there were persistent whispers when Supergirl Li Yuchun gyrated like a tomboy: Is she a lesbian? Is she bisexual? Time magazine crowned her an "Asian hero", though not necessarily on the basis of her sexual politics: Li Yuchun has always been timid in discussing her androgynous demeanor.

Nevertheless, thousands of Li Yuchun wannabes soon emerged – people who disguised their gender so well that it would take a medical examination to be sure. And now it has come full circle: *My Hero* is presenting a corps of men remarkable for their delicate looks, soft voices and accessorizing skills. The television contest, organized by Shanghai Media Group, professionally known as SMG, and broadcast on the Shanghai Satellite Station, features young men out-singing, out-dancing and out-courting one another to the screams and tears of a legion of teenage girls.

Their singing is even shakier than that of the *Supergirl* champion. But one area where they out-shine the female contestants of the rival show is in the arena of beauty.

Some in the audience complain they are too sissy; others suggest they might be gay or tailored for a gay audience. But that is tantamount to Bush's "You are either with us or against us" logic. These young men are marching to the drum of diminishing sexual identity. They are beyond gay or straight. Truth is, the object of their love is themselves. In other words, they are China's first generation of self-conscious metrosexuals, even though the word does not have a Chinese equivalent yet and the concept is still making its rounds in glossy magazines.

The storm whipped up by *My Hero* is not really a twister. The fascination with "beautiful men" was most popular in the Ming Dynasty (1368-1644) and metrosexual idols have long been touted by Chinese entertainment editors, who post photos of male celebrities in self-obsessed poses from Rudolf

Young man, you've come to the wrong place

Supergirl

Valentino to Leslie Cheung.

The most obvious influence on the androgynous look that is in vogue today may be Japanese anime, where a typical hero is a youth with big eyes, flowing hair and a supple and slender physique.

Some male audience members hate the show. One from Nanjing even threatened to organize a boycott if the show did not vote out an 18-year-old who has been called "the male counterpart of Li Yuchun".

It does not take a sociologist to know that most voters for *Supergirls* or *My Hero* are young women. Their choice of men or women goes against conventional wisdom, which – come to think of it – is codified by men. In a male-dominated society, the ideal men are supposed to be macho, and women, well, feminine. In the early 1980s, we had Japanese actor Ken Takakura, a man of few words who captured the hearts of millions of Chinese. But nowadays women want men who can communicate and be gentle and loving. They also want someone who can fill their emotional need for giving love.

One of the hottest "heroes" is an orphan who lost his mother at the age of six, while another has lost hearing and speaking abilities. They do not seem to have any outstanding talent, but are sweet and vulnerable, with good looks to boot. Women go crazy for them. They are the perfect object for motherly or sisterly affection.

It deals a heavy blow to the traditional image of man as the head of the household, the protector who would stare down the threat of the villain. If the two television reality shows are any indication, it seems we are on the threshold of an era when women will not need to be porcelain dolls and men will spend a lot more time grooming themselves.

The metrosexual male fits the role to a tee. He can wear jewelry without being suspected of being a drama queen. He can put on an air of calculated casualness that tells women that he cares without looking obsequious. The appearance of this type of man will elevate the art of courtship, no matter how much other men hate it.

Thanks to Li Yuchun and SMG's *My Hero*, sexual politics in China may no longer be what it used to be.

41. Don't judge December-May romances

February 11, 2006

Come Valentine's Day, shop windows and magazine covers will display perfectly matched pairs happy in love. And one of the "perfections" is compatibility in age. Simply put, the guy should be slightly older than the gal. As the old saying goes, "if the man is older by three years, there'll be golden nuggets in store for the couple."

But we live in an imperfect world. Or rather, the "imperfections" make our world so colorful. Extreme conformity usually signifies terrible things. That doesn't mean everyone accepts May-December affairs – those between an older man and younger women – without raising an eyebrow now and then.

When 82-year-old Nobel Prize winner Chen Ning Yang married 28-year-old Weng Fan, it made a tidal wave in a teacup. Even those who usually refrained from being judgmental could not help jumping in the fray.

A 54-year gap may be a bit hard for many to swallow, but in recent years the male lead in age is expanding way beyond the three-year golden rule of thumb, as wealthy people who have made it, usually in their middle age, marry those much younger.

Whispers of trophy wives or gold diggers abound. But the phenomenon is by no means confined to present-day China. It is a throwback to the old days when men with money and power took in concubine after concubine whose age barely put them over the legal limit.

When someone reverses the May-December formula to December-May under this social background, it takes on a revolutionary simulacrum and subverts male-domination in sexual politics. And the celebrities in the entertainment industry are the ones who have blazed the trail in the past decade and made "*jie di lian*" (love between an older woman and a younger man) an acceptable – or at least not unthinkable – notion. Fay Wong's on-again, off-again entanglement with the iconic Nicolas Tse, which lasted longer than many had predicted, helped turn "*jie di lian*" into a trend.

In the US, no fortune-teller forecast longevity for Demi Moore and Ashton Kutcher, with a 15-year age gap, whose two-year courtship culminated in marriage. When they first started dating, the consensus opinion interpreted it as a publicity stunt.

When people date out of their "age league" so to speak, eyebrows are always raised. What's the motive? How could a man young enough to be a woman's son want her to be his lifetime Valentine? Is it her money, status, power?

And as for her, why does she want a boy-toy when she could have someone her own age? Is it an attempt to capture her fading youth, an illusion of mistaking wealth for sex appeal or simply a disguise of keeping a gigolo?

Some of these questions are legitimate, but only for family members and close friends to ask. As long as the two people involved are consenting adults, they know what they are getting into, pitfalls and all. What rights do we, as outsiders, have to play God or psychoanalyst, for that matter?

When we pass judgment on an unconventional relationship, we are using either a set code of conduct that we deem decorous or lessons from similar stories that happened in the past. But one December-May fling embedded in deceit and exploitation does not mean all such pairings are like that.

And who is in a position to decree what reverse age difference is befitting? The old saying is sometimes turned around to accommodate an older woman dating a younger man. But who says the cut-off has to be three years?

Love, just like deceit and exploitation, finds itself into every possible combination of age, height, hobby and status. But the stigma surrounding love still seems to be different.

A survey shows that single women over 30 have the hardest time finding a spouse, especially when they have successful careers. A quote by a survey participant illustrates: "He has to be older than I am, even by one day. He has to be taller than I am, even by one inch, and he has to make more than I do, even by one yuan."

The cruel truth is, men who qualify for this ideal beau tend to be either happily married or looking for May-December amours. For these women, who reportedly account for 70 percent of the reluctant urban singles, a December-May match should not be a self-imposed taboo. They should follow their hearts and take risks, and who knows, love may blossom in the most unlikely places.

42. Forget date rental for new year

February 09, 2007

This could be the premise for a romantic comedy: Someone who pays for a date falls head over heels in love with that person and they end up walking into the sunset hand in hand.

In reality, the yarn with Chinese characteristics has only Act I, which usually makes it into headlines and raises a few eyebrows. Many are curious what happens after boy meets girl, but the press does not seem to investigate further.

In the past few years, some young people – mostly men and often college students – find themselves under pressure to bring their sweethearts on their journey home for the all-important Spring Festival. Mom and Dad want to meet their future son/daughter-in-law. If you don't have a steady but are eager to please your folks, the only option is to have someone pretend to be the loved one.

Now, we've heard of hiring maids or interior designers. Renting a date, albeit for a noble purpose, sounds dubious. People suspect this could be a decoy for

seeking prostitution. They wonder how the couple travel and whether they share a room. Well, those who raise doubts probably won't say it, but that's what is troubling them.

You see, people like to worry about certain things. A generation ago, they feared that social dancing could lead to a surge in extramarital affairs. When a man and a woman who are not married touch each others' hands, where would it lead to? Will their physical contact go one step further? This line of thinking will go all the way to childbearing, the inerasable testament of the encounter of a certain kind.

This is not nosiness of select individuals. It is in our genes and sanctified in Confucius' *Analects*. We just cannot bring ourselves to admit that this is none of our business. But as long as people in the arrangement are consenting adults and do not break any laws, posing as someone's fiancé does not really warrant our moral scrutiny.

The real victims are the parents, who are also enforcers of another age-old code of tradition: namely, children should marry and bear children, preferably as early as possible. Chinese parents just cannot accept the notion that their children are independent human beings with the right to choose their own lifestyle; and whether and when they marry are their own business.

Luckily, we no longer live in a time of arranged marriage when parents picked spouses for their children and those entering matrimony did not see each other until the night of the wedding. I wouldn't say Chinese parents are selfish, but they insist certain things be done in certain ways. They are observing old customs rather than thinking for the benefit of their children. That's why those who enjoy the DINK (Dual Income No Kids) lifestyle or are homosexuals who do not want sham marriages find themselves in extremely difficult positions.

However, those who hire dates may not belong to these categories. They just want their parents to be happy and proud. If everyone else is accompanied by a girlfriend, why shouldn't I?

It's one more manifestation of catching up with the Joneses. The herd mentality surfaces in all age groups. The young want to show off their presumably urbanized companions, and the old want to flaunt the success of their offspring – their girlfriends, new accents, new gadgets and all.

If someone makes a movie with this plot, it is likely that the parents will see through the charade and say something like "As long as you're happy, I'm happy for you." In reality, nobody will be enlightened this way, and the money used for renting the date will be money down the drain.

Note: Unbeknownst to me, a movie based on such a plot was in the making. Contract Lover *was released in late 2007 and was not a hit.*

43. Maid in China

November 11, 2006

Maids make up a big segment in China's labor market. Many middle-class families employ them, freeing wage-earners from household chores and helping balance the economy by allowing their wealth to trickle down.

Recently, a labor market in Shaanxi Province has been advertising a special kind of maid, who not only takes care of cooking and cleaning, but offers "bed-sharing" services with the head of the household. According to the ad, these maids tend to be from rural areas – a totally redundant description since almost all maids have rural backgrounds – are over 35 years old and earn a high 2,000 yuan (US$250) a month, in a market where a regular maid's pay is about 500 yuan (US$60).

As one can imagine, the moral warriors are jumping up and down in a carnival of denunciation. Some have suggested the police "monitor" employer-maid relations.

I don't know how that can be done. Does it mean police should barge into families with maids, at midnight, unannounced, as they used to do in hotels? To make that proposal feasible, anyone who hires a maid will have to surrender his privacy.

According to one dubious survey, around 5 percent of maids have sex with their employers. Is that something we should tolerate? It all depends on the circumstances. In most cases, it is the result of sexual harassment. Even though things happen within the confines of a private space, it is not different in nature from advances in an office environment.

The top priority is for those in this line of work to be aware of the potential "occupational hazard" and learn how to protect themselves. It is the job of employment agencies to educate them beforehand and the duty of women's associations to intervene whenever maids report such incidents.

Now I don't believe most employers are sex maniacs. They may be tempted, but when they know their maids are armed with legal knowledge and understand where to draw the line, they will back down and behave. The Shaanxi case, if the report is accurate, is another story. Though widely considered immoral, this act, in my opinion, is less despicable than preying on the uninitiated.

We have to see this in the proper social context. Prostitution, albeit illegal, is rampant under umpteen guises. More relevant is *"ernai"*, a uniquely Chinese phenomenon whereby a man takes a second wife and stashes her away in another abode.

Police may have periodic crackdown on prostitution, but nobody has heard of a vice squad against *ernai* unless it involves an official who falls from grace. The relationship is not legally protected, but people seem to have a tacit understanding about what would otherwise be put in a prenuptial agreement.

The Shaanxi "bed-sharing" maid is just a variation on the high-priced Pearl River Delta kind, a poor man's *ernai*. We wish these women were jolted out of contentment and fought for their legal rights. But whatever vestige of feminism they may have, it is foiled by the strong pull of commercialism.

Granted, the Shaanxi ad should not have existed. It is a sad reminder of the dynamic chaos we live in today. It testifies to the yawning wealth gap, the insufficiency of decent jobs, and the need for empowering women to protect themselves. However, it would be a cop-out to clean up the ad and punish the advertiser, while sweeping the fundamental issues under the rug.

44. Sex sells, but tastefulness still vital

Macrch 25, 2006

In China, sexual politics tends to play out in operatic overindulgence. Posturing and scenery-chewing are the norm. Subtlety is not something to be appreciated.

First, a recent spate of the glaring maneuver:

In Shanghai, a real estate exhibition hired topless women, their bare bodies strategically painted with flowery patterns, to sell housing units.

In the Northeastern city of Changchun, one restaurant owner came up with the idea of asking her waitresses to wear menu tags on their breasts.

Talk about the "eyeball economy". Once you unleash the entrepreneurship, the creativity is unbounded.

The counter-maneuvers are equally heavy-handed.

In Wuxi, a city in East China's Jiangsu Province, local education authorities decreed that no teacher should be left alone with a student of the opposite sex. It is meant to prevent male teachers from sexually harassing female students, media reports emphasized.

But one cannot help wondering: What if a conversation starts with two students and then one of them has to leave? Should the teacher excuse himself rather than continuing to talk with the single female student? What if the teacher is gay and is more likely to be physically attracted to male students? Should the pronouncement be revised to include scenarios of any sexual orientation?

Human society is complicated. Laws and ethics exist to regulate our behavior, but generalizing a whole group of people as potential victimizers is to use a cow knife to kill a chicken. Granted, there have been numerous reports of teachers molesting girls. Some of the cases were so heinous, such as the one who raped his students right in the back of the classroom or the one who demanded young girls go to his office one by one, that it is simply beyond comprehension for people living in vigilant urban areas.

But ever since Confucius' time, teaching has been a noble profession. The public holds teachers in high esteem. The few rotten apples among them should not turn the whole group into a target of suspicion.

Given that teachers probably already know what is proper when it comes to making contact with students, it's the students, especially the underaged, who should receive awareness training on how to protect themselves. They should be told explicitly that they have recourse if they suspect any inappropriate behavior by a teacher, or a fellow student for that matter.

This will be like American kids who threaten to call the cops and allege child abuse when their parents are about to spank them.

The Changchun restaurant reminds me of Hooters, the US restaurant chain that employs big-breasted waitresses who wear tight T-shirts. The objectification of women in both cases is obvious. But somehow, with Hooters, it's more unpretentious, while the practice of menu tags is a bit sneaky and hypocritical. To fend off criticism, the restaurant owner asked her male employees to do the same. But feminists must be crying foul: It's just not the same for men to wear something on their chests.

There's no denying that sex appeal sells. It is not unhealthy in itself. One should overcome the stigma of outdated moral codes and appreciate it for what it is. But in breaking loose of the shackles, some have opted for lasciviousness and cheap thrills. That has created situations that not only run against public acceptance, but are counterproductive in themselves.

Take the body-paint models at the trade show. They no doubt drew in a bigger crowd, but the crowd was fixated on the titillating parts of the female bodies rather than the glowing miniatures of high-rises.

There is a similarity with fashion designer Versace using stunning human forms, usually au naturel, to sell fashion products. But housing is not the same as haute couture. Are you more likely to buy an apartment because a stark naked model-type inhabited a similar unit?

The trick is to use sex appeal tastefully. There are non-exploitive ways to associate a product or service with sex appeal and it takes more imagination than parading flesh.

45. Adult humor has its place among mature

February 25, 2006

Let's face it: The popularity of short messaging in China has a dirty little secret. It's called "adult humor", more plainly known as sex jokes.

It is almost stereotype-busting that Chinese, who are portrayed in the West as either spouting Confucian epithets or burying heads in books, could have fun with this kind of jokes. But in the past decade it has been an undercurrent of urban culture.

Of course, not everyone enjoys it. Some are appalled. I was one of them when I first came back from years of work and study overseas as a "sea turtle". A friend of mine was putting out naughty dispatches that were more explicit than funny, and he did not seem to care who was in the audience, kids or colleagues.

I agree that, after decades of moral whipping, we Chinese need to loosen up a little, and some verbal horseplay is harmless. However, everything depends on the occasion. I don't see anything wrong with sharing dirty jokes within an intimate circle of friends. It's human

nature.

On other occasions, it could be definitely inappropriate. For example, you won't banter in sexual puns with your parents or your children. In simple words, one should not share adult humor with anyone who, for whatever reason, is uncomfortable with it. That sounds like common sense.

The new public security law, to be enacted in March, is necessary. It stipulates that anyone who repeatedly sends words of a sexual, insulting or threatening nature to harass others could be arrested. The maximum penalty for the offence is five to 10 days in jail and up to a 500-yuan fine. I hope it deters those few sick minds who use adult humor to exert psychological coercion on others.

But for most people who use this kind of witticism to create a congenial and close-knit atmosphere, the new law hopefully should not become a wet blanket. Law enforcement officials should not act as moral arbiters and mistake those with occasional improper remarks for those with ulterior motives.

It reminds me of the mid-1990s during the immediate aftermath of the Clarence Thomas-Anita Hill scandal. Many US companies, fearful of sexual harassment lawsuits, hired outside consultants to lecture employees about what's proper and what's not in an office environment.

The one I sat through basically concluded that anything a male employee might say to a female employee could be interpreted as sexual harassment, even if it's just a compliment on her new dress. After several tedious sessions of such "political indoctrination", I heard some of the Silicon Valley geeks whispering "Nazis" to the brain-washers' backs.

It was a classic case of good intention gone wrong. And that was in a nation where adult jokes – the mild kind – are frequently employed in films and television shows.

In China, adult humor is confined to its grassroots where mobile phones, instant messaging and word of mouth are the main platforms. The boundaries of propriety are observed by individual intuition rather than a collective consciousness.

But we are honing our skills. Even the recent CCTV Spring Festival Gala included a sexual one-liner, when the Chinese word for "specialty" (*te chang*) was uttered in such an ambiguous way that adults caught on, children were oblivious and those it embarrassed could choose to ignore it.

It is a sign of maturity that humor and witticism of any kind are customized for their target audiences, rather than used indiscriminately or banned.

46. Hong Kong sex scandal

February 23, 2008

There are many ways to interpret the sex photo scandal of Hong Kong pop stars. But the core of the matter, as I see it, is the wrangling between the law and morality.

On the legal side, it is not hard to pinpoint who broke the law. If you take your notebook computer to a repair shop and the repairman makes a copy of your hard drive without your permission, that is

stealing, pure and simple. For those netizens who disagree, let me give an analogy: Say you call a cable repairman to your home to fix the line, and he gets curious about the contents of your closet and removes something, that would be against any rule of ethics or law. There is no way you can explain it away by saying you stumbled upon it or the item you took could be incriminating evidence against the customer.

If the repairman happened to notice Edison Chen's photos – the actor at the center of the scandal – which he felt were immoral or illegal, he should have called the authorities instead of snooping around other people's private lives.

What Chen did with his lovers was not illegal if (a) the women were not coerced, (b) they were not underage when the photos were taken, or (c) he did not intend to publicize the photos. From what we know now, it seems to be the case. So, from a legal perspective, Chen and the starlets were victims.

Yet, when you search and research online, the predominant reaction is against Chen, and not the one who filched his digital files. That is because the digital thief did not seem to have any commercial or malicious intention. He just shared his loot with some friends, and one of them could not resist the temptation to share it with the vast online populace.

It is obviously inappropriate to spread photos of such a private nature, but one cannot equate the human weakness of curiosity with the deliberate violation of the law. If anyone who has looked at the images has broken the law, there would not be a prison large enough to hold all the offenders.

The Hong Kong police belatedly tried to draw a fine line between those who share with friends and those who transmit indiscriminately, but it only turned the incident into an endless stream of titillation. Moreover, by actively prosecuting the case, the Hong Kong police caused a backlash from netizens who accused the police of selective enforcement of the law: Why do you go after a few net users while everything was initiated by the star? They argued.

True, Chen and his bedfellows should help the police in their investigations, but what they did falls mostly into the moral realm. The licentiousness may have caught many by surprise. That is because ordinary people were duped by the giant machine of the entertainment industry, which excels at fabricating the public personas of pop idols.

Chen is portrayed as a nice, wholesome boy and Gillian Chung, one half of the singing duo, The Twins, as an innocent girl who believes in chastity before marriage. Those who believe this are simply fools. Wake up! What you see is just roles they play.

You would be disillusioned if you see them as role models. Many are not, except for their good looks. I do not sympathize with them because when they get into the business of being an idol, they implicitly follow the rules and play their roles, agreed or thrust upon them. If they play fast and loose, they must be held responsible for the occupational hazards that may ensue.

The age of innocence has long gone. This scandal only makes it clearer.

Chapter Eight
Highbrow and Lowbrow

47. Arts events for national holidays

October 01, 2005

I once flew over a sprawling metropolis in the American South on the night of July 4. Small pockets of fireworks sparkled below, many of which I knew were illegal. Unknown to many Chinese, US cities also have strict policies on firecrackers and organize periodic crackdowns on unauthorized selling and using. And like in China, the restrictions don't work that well.

People want an outlet for their jubilation and firecrackers, for all the obvious side effects, seem to provide for this. Of course, the Chinese, except Hongkongers, don't usually stage firework displays on the National Day. They are usually saved for the Lunar New Year.

Mainland Chinese have something for our National Day that nobody else has: a weeklong holiday. But before it becomes the envy of the world, it has run into a few glitches, most notably traffic jams at tourist sites. Tens of millions of people taking to the road and cramming into national parks and world heritage sites can strain resources beyond the capacity of any business. So how can a country of 1.3 billion have a collective celebration without creating chaos or resorting to such extreme action as holding a series of rehearsed events?

One solution is to offer diversified live entertainment by organizing for the nation's performing arts troupes to stage outdoor public events.

As more and more urbanites are staying away from popular tourist destinations, cities are swarming with people during the Golden Week. Citizens may take short getaways, call on friends or relax at home, where they have time to go on shopping trips or jaunts to local parks. Millions of migrant workers, in particular, won't be leaving cities because of the expense of doing so and having fewer days off.

All this creates perfect conditions for staging small-sized public performances across metropolitan China. And these shows should be free and publicized. If prepared well, they would entail very little marginal cost or logistics.

China's performing arts troupes are almost all state-sponsored. In return, they offer a certain number of "non-commercial" performances by traveling to remote rural areas or industrial towns to add a "taste of culture". But they also spend time on elaborate acts that appeal to only a few award jurors.

If each of these groups put on a single full-length show during the 7-day holiday in a public venue such as a park, a downtown plaza or a closed-off street, it could easily draw an audience of thousands, many of whom will be in search of recreational activities to kill their time. It doesn't have to be elaborate, just two-dozen singers, dancers and comedians with proper sound amplification on a slightly elevated makeshift stage – voila, we have a show. And it doesn't have to be specially programmed as existing acts from their repertories may fit the bill perfectly.

Offering free performances on the street can enliven a city's cultural scene with the minimum amount of investment. And it won't encroach on arts groups' regular business because it's basically a free sampling of their "products" and will most probably entice more paying patrons in the future.

Yet, many artists will cringe at such a prospect. Performing arts are sacred to them, and a properly outfitted theater is the only setting they'll find acceptable. Ever since New China exalted the status of performing artists, it inadvertently set up a partition between those who perform and those who watch. It seems art is to be delivered from up high. Singing, dancing, telling jokes and doing somersaults among the audience, rather in front of them and on the street, may remind one of street performers of the old days who were essentially beggars.

But it doesn't have to be that way. In the West, free performances go on all through summer. Opera companies and classical orchestras dole out popular offerings. Even Meryl Streep gives her rendition of classic plays in New York's Central Park, turning it into the cultural event of the year for that city.

Now, imagine an ancient capital like Beijing, where performing arts troupes may exceed 100. One free outdoor performance by each company, preferably for each of the three Golden Weeks or, better, spread throughout the year, will make Beijing one of the most culturally vibrant places in the world, and leave many holiday-weary residents and visitors humming a happy tune.

48. Grand National Theater. Can you afford it?

January 05, 2008

I know a lot of people don't agree with me, but I've always believed in the necessity of building a Grand National Theater in China. Yes, in terms of marginal benefit, the money would probably have been better spent on rural education or poverty alleviation. But a nation as culturally rich as China needs a venue worthy of its performing arts.

Besides, if we recovered a little bit of government waste, money would have been no problem anyway.

I was involved in an early phase of the feasibility study for the theater around 20 years ago, when I took a group of experts on tour along the West Coast of the United States. They were on a mission to evaluate offerings in the US as they prepared plans for the future national theater. We visited several old theaters in downtown San Francisco as well as its historically important opera house. We drove down to Los Angeles to explore more performing arts halls. The one in Orange County does not have any right angles, we were told.

Nothing I saw on that trip prepared me for what just opened next to the Great Hall of the People. I know the design is controversial, but it's so much better than the other designs that made it into the final competition. I'm no architect, but I believe the best architecture risks becoming just a landmark for tourism if it does not function properly.

By "function" I mean presenting great art on its three stages.

The first signs are encouraging. It seems the theater is not destined to overtake the Great Hall as a setting for politically themed performances. It could so easily have been a place where every province showcases its achievements by staging its own variety shows.

The Grand National Theater drew a lot of press coverage when it started selling standing tickets. Costing just 30 yuan each, the 100 tickets attracted a phalanx of huddled masses, some of whom had queued throughout the night.

Grand National Theater

I sympathize with them. A decade ago, I snapped up a lot of standing tickets at the San Francisco Opera. I called them "student tickets" because only financially destitute students like me would be willing to stand for a five-hour Wagner opera. Sometimes, when the action on stage came to a standstill, I – and a few fellow standees – would sit down on the floor and just enjoy the glorious music wafting across the hall.

Standing tickets, in my opinion, are the cheapest way to nurture the next generation of classical music lovers. Over here, some pundits see them as further proof of the rich-poor divide. In San Francisco, I was never treated badly because the opera house knew many of us would one day graduate to regular patrons.

Once I came back to China, I found – to my dismay – tickets so overpriced that most of the people who go to the theater are either institutional ticket buyers or complimentary ticket holders. A lavish show costs money. In the West, a show runs for hundreds, even thousands, of days, while here in China a week is considered a long run. You do the math.

Since the initial production cost is fixed, why not lower the price and run longer so that more people have a chance to be exposed to the magic of the theater? Hopefully the Grand National Theater can create some competition and provide more access to people who otherwise cannot afford to go, even the standing tickets.

As an aside, an acquaintance of mine told me he had come up with the English name the National Center for Performing Arts. It is similar to Lincoln Center or Kennedy Center. But would it replace the more habitual moniker or create confusion? Maybe it'll be best known by its nickname, the Giant Egg.

49. Best comedy knows how to tickle audience

June 09, 2007

When you visit a Northeastern city like Shenyang or Changchun, you've got to catch a show of "*er ren zhuan*" (two-person act), a local form of standup comedy, singing and acrobatic stunts all rolled into one. It is becoming as de rigueur as a Broadway show is to a traveler to New York.

Unlike most theater entertainment you'll encounter in China, the "*er ren zhuan*" performances are not funded by the state, nor do they feature a battalion of performers with diplomas from vocational schools. In my mind, that is why they fill the house night after night.

For much of the past several decades, performing arts in China have been a kind of "official affair", with performers on government payroll and programs reflecting government policies rather than public sentiments.

Since the 1980s, these flowers of the "arts" have been withering. Occasionally, a troupe invests a few million yuan of taxpayers' money to put on a new show, which would be performed half a dozen times, get some awards from government agencies, find itself into somebody's work report of grand achievement and then fold forever.

As virtually none of its audiences are actual ticket-buyers, the show would reap only so-called "social benefits", a euphemism for losing one's pants financially but pleasing some higher-ranking officials. Truth be told, it is not devoid of artistic merit. It is just detached from the needs of ordinary people, including the high-brow ones.

Then, there are the wild flowers of grassroots entertainment, forms like "*er ren zhuan*" in the Northeast and Shaoxing Opera in Zhejiang. They tend to blossom not because of – but despite – government intervention. They may not be as polished as the routines by professional performers, but they make people laugh and cry, which is what good entertainment is all about.

Some officials have the mistaken notion that arts and entertainment are all about prettily decked-out singers warbling praises of the latest official slogans that are in fad. They present squeaky-clean images and simulated joys. Like postcard sceneries, they are better to be marveled at than embraced with your heart.

If the official entertainment is like the powdered face of an aristocrat, grassroots entertainment is like the sweaty face of a young man toiling in the field. It may be gritty, but full of vitality and closer to life as we know it. The Northeastern comedy draws much of its gags from daily life. Unfortunately, the show I caught has already been "purified" due to censorship pressure.

Traditional "*er ren zhuan*" has bawdy jokes galore. That may get into trouble with censors who have obviously never read such literary classics as Chaucer's *Canterbury Tales* or Boccaccio's *Decameron*. So, the performers adopted a "greening" strategy, removing much of the R-rated banter, flushing away some of the boisterous vigor in the process.

My friends told me that if I want to catch a show with "original flavor", I'd have to venture out of downtown and into makeshift venues where roving performers have not yet caught the attention of authorities.

Pressures have also been growing on text-message jokes, one of the few remaining platforms where ordinary people can invent something funny and share with friends. Granted, there are messages that should not be sent unsolicited. But as long as the sender does not act out of malice, this is the cellphone equivalent of a silent "*er ren zhuan*" moment.

The best comedians may not be properly educated or certified, and may not be government sanctioned, but they know how to tickle an audience. Comedy, like all live entertainment, cannot thrive in an over-regulated environment. The more comedy is "*greened*", the less it'll be relevant to our times.

50. Festival gala as tasteless as chicken ribs

January 27, 2006

Tomorrow night is the eve of Spring Festival – the Lunar New Year when hundreds of millions of Chinese families sit around a table and take in the year-end feast and the heart-warming atmosphere of family reunion. In the past 23 years, this ritual has been accompanied by a television show that has metamorphosed into the mother of all shows.

The Spring Festival Eve Gala on China Central Television (CCTV) is a variety show that features singing, dancing and comedy skits. It is very long, spanning four or five hours, and has a cast of thousands, all trying very hard to put on their best smile lest someone doubts their joyous spirit. As the highest-rated TV show in China and one of the highest worldwide, it may be the most reviled anywhere, judging from the usual outpouring of post-show panning and sneering.

Last year, only one number was considered an unqualified success: "Thousand-Hand Guanyin" (the Goddess of Mercy dance) by an ensemble of disabled performers. I was not a bit surprised. I had seen the same dance in Hong Kong and overseas by the same troupe and it was always greeted with tears and applause. But CCTV's producers trimmed it almost to a snippet.

Most years, not a single number would stand out. The songs tend to be derivative, the dances generic, the comedy stale and the laughter from the live audience orchestrated. There is a segment called "Reading telegrams and telephone messages", which is de rigueur but hated by almost everyone: Who in this age of mobile phones and email would send New Year greetings in Morse code? And who can possibly get through to the CCTV hotline?

Even the show's set is more chinoiserie than Chinese, with visual symbols piled one after another into a jumble. The joy of festivities does not seem to flow naturally, but rather, pumped out by a pedestrian craftsman stealing every trick from the Zhang Yimou color factory.

Everything about the show is not only top of the line, but over the top. In a sense, it's become the ultimate kitsch show – all high camp and no spontaneity. The performers have been rehearsed to

death; the songs are pre-recorded, and the jokes lack any bite. Yet, we cannot spend the last few hours of the lunar year without it. We love to hate it because we expect so much, sometimes unreasonably. Many call it "chicken rib", worthless to keep, but a pity to throw away.

Back in 1983 when the show was first launched, not every family had a television set, and nightlife was non-existent. It was literally watched by everyone who had a TV. The show brought genuine laughter and a communal sense of enjoyment. Honestly speaking, the shows for the first couple of years were not that good. There were few production values. The pacing was terrible. But no matter. People had only good memories of it because we didn't expect much. In a sense, the show became a victim of its own runaway success.

By the end of the 1980s, the gala was already an institution, as indispensable to the New Year's Eve celebration as firecrackers. As such, it cannot possibly live up to public anticipation. As it grows more lavish in production, the content itself has got into so deep a rut that an eight-horse cart cannot pull it out.

As CCTV is the only national network, all television channels at provincial level simply look up to it and produce their own mini-galas, which are pale imitations.

However, it would be simplistic to criticize CCTV for not trying. It's constantly tinkering with the format, importing token Hong Kong and Taiwan entertainers to spruce things up. But they are constrained exactly because the show is such a juggernaut and any change would bring about unexpected (or expected) complaints. It is supposed to entertain everyone, but as our society diversifies in taste, there is simply not a single number or a single show that can satisfy everyone.

51. Too much TV not a good thing

March 01, 2008

Call me snobbish, but I have never hidden my disappointment with Chinese television. In general, that is. I am not ruling out the occasional decent show.

When I flip through the 60-some channels, I rarely stumble upon anything to my taste. Not educational programming like Discovery or PBS. For that, I have to trek to a certain stall in southern China, whose owner has a warehouse of great discs.

Recently, I got a box set of Kenneth Clark's *Civilization*, a BBC series that functioned as the "open sesame" to a world of Western civilization for me, while I was a graduate student in Guangzhou, in the early 1980s. Maria Jaschok, my German-born English professor borrowed canisters of films from the British Embassy and for the first time I realized that great art does not necessarily spring from class struggle.

Sure, CCTV10, as well as an array of imitators, is attempting to fill this void. Its runaway hit The *Lecture Room* does a service to various aspects of Chinese culture. But a lecture filled with graphics and footage from period dramas does not equal a good documentary with high production values. And focusing on only a few Chinese classics does not make what Francis Bacon called "a full man". Why not broaden the vista to embrace other fields, such as modern Chinese literature, or French Impressionist paintings, or Shakespeare?

Speaking of production values, Chinese soap operas have come a long way from the not-too-distant past of shabby costumes and haphazard lighting. But I can hardly bear to put myself through a whole show because I can tell from the first episode what will happen by the grand finale. Worse, whenever a character says his or her line, it is easy for me to predict the follow-up line.

Last month, the publicist of a television company sent me a copy of a high-prestige new show to critique. When he called me up, I said: "Congratulations on a potential hit!"

"So, you liked it," he said.

"No way. I watched only the first hour and it's so formulaic I could quickly tell who would end up with whom by the end. My mother-in-law loved it, though. She is a better barometer. If I loved your show, it would probably bomb as no middle-aged housewives would swoon with joy or anguish at the melodrama."

As I see it, Chinese television entertainment is a paragon of kitsch, especially as far as variety shows are concerned. When last summer CCTV let ethnic singers use their "original style", audiences were stunned: singing without the pretense of overheated emoting, or so-called professional training, could touch our hearts like a force of nature.

You can imagine why it made me laugh when I saw the proclamation this week that China is now officially "the biggest producing and broadcasting country of television drama". Last year we churned out 40 episodes a day, some of which were aired on 90 percent of the country's 1,974 channels.

Now, I don't expect every show to be smart and witty and thought provoking, but just like Hollywood blockbusters, our television programming seems to aim for the lowest common denominator.

For those of you who rely on your tube as a language tool, I have this advice: We Chinese don't actually talk like that in real life. What you see is a parallel universe populated by eerily hollow characters, such as 20-somethings who spend a fortune on a meal or otherwise act with no discernable motive.

52. Don't parade entertainers as role models

October 29, 2005

The dumbing down of China is on an inexorable course.

Recently, a German television show reported that China's television lacks educational programming. No surprise here. China may be deficient in many things, but one thing it has in abundance is entertainment information. If you care to browse an urban daily or turn to most television channels, you would think that, instead of 100 million-plus migrant workers, we have 100 million entertainers.

Don't get me wrong. I'm not against entertainment programming per se. On the contrary, I believe it serves a purpose in the grand scheme of things: takes pressure off our daily lives by turning our minds temporarily to trivia; satisfies our voyeuristic instincts; and provides us common topics for idle chat.

For a while in our history, entertainment was taboo. Thirty years ago, there were no movie-star posters; and 40 years ago, movie-star posters in cinemas had to be approved by the authorities. But when entertainment news resurfaced, it came back with a vengeance.

But proliferation does not breed professionalism. For all the inundation of star gossip, much of it is thinly veiled public relations releases. Reporters are frequently paid off with red envelopes and are easily and willingly manipulated by celebrities of a certain status. Those with no access to big names, especially some local tabloids, routinely resort to fabricating stories out of thin air or do quick copy-and-paste jobs from online postings.

But who am I to complain about the low standard? Readers and audiences are devouring whatever is offered them. The target of these "products" is young adults, who tend to be gullible and in need of idols.

The job of an entertainer is to entertain. I don't mean to disparage, but they should not be looked up as gods. Because of ubiquitous exposure, which is built-in with the job, many are perceived as having halos around them. Most fans grow out of this phase, but not some officials and authorities of

prestigious universities. Therein lies the rub.

Hong Kong superstar Andy Lau made an appearance at Fudan University's centennial celebration. Granted, Lau is known for his versatility and has been somewhat of a role model, but he is not a Fudan alumnus, nor does he have any other association with the school. His "gig" did bring more coverage from the press, but the focus was on the star, not the school.

Peking University invites so many pop celebrities that, if you depend solely on website news, you'd be forgiven to conclude that this is not an esteemed institution of higher learning but a busy fan club.

I'm not so snobbish as to imply that entertainers should not be allowed as guest speakers. They have their areas of expertise, such as acting, singing and performing, and may well share their knowledge and insight with college students. But they are often pressed for deep thoughts on life, philosophy and other grand topics. In fact, schools use them more as baits of attraction than experts in their own fields.

Stephen Chow, the reigning king of comedy, has made his round of Beijing schools, but he admitted that he was aware of the ludicrousness of it all. Jet Li, who recently gave a lecture at Peking University, felt he was not qualified to speak there because he did not even have a primary-school education.

Besides administrators of top schools, county officials in remote areas are also among the star-struck. Some of them spend a big chunk of their annual revenues just to get a few stars to dress up an event, while oblivious to the widespread poverty still existing in their jurisdiction.

Singing and acting are professions. Just like others, a few of the practitioners make it big time, even fewer become role models and once in a blue moon, a national hero may emerge. Some mistake their public personas for their genuine selves. By elevating them beyond their capacity, such as giving them the task of college administration or enshrining them in textbooks, one is taking the fish out of the water – a disservice to both the fish and the fish consumer.

Let entertainers be confined to entertainment pages.

53. Dabbling in real politics

March 08, 2008

As we all know, politics can be entertaining, and the entertainment business is full of politics. But when entertainers get into real politics, it raises eyebrows.

Every time China's two Sessions get into full swing, a handful of entertainment celebrities are thrust into the spotlight – not for their achievements in their own fields, but for the way they represent their industry in the National People's Congress (NPC) and the Chinese People's Political Consultative Conference (CPPCC).

If I were a member sitting next to them, I would be ignored by all the reporters swarming around the movie stars and big-name directors. But you cannot blame the media. What Gong Li or Feng Xiaogang blurt out will certainly arouse more interest from many readers than, say, the three unknowns who represent China's 100-million-plus migrant workers.

Our society is poisoned by celebrity worship. Reputations, good or bad, have monetary value. Like it or not, the bigger the names, the more weight their words carry. At least more influence. Viewed in another context, it is the result of more openness in public discourse. Imagine the movie stars repeating lines from a prepared script endorsed by their superiors.

So, do not laugh at Gong Li last year filing a motion titled "Environmental protection should start with me". Yes, it sounds like a schoolgirl's essay assignment, but it is clear she meant what she wrote.

We should understand that these high-profile stars are taking baby steps in the initial stage of a political process called democracy. They were not born with the talent to study social issues or sift through public opinion. Unlike their professional performances, which are edited or rehearsed for the best possible result, climbing up the learning curve in the Great Hall of the People, in front of a cluster of cameras and microphones, can be awkward.

Fortunately, more of them come prepared. Feng Xiaogang, director of many hit movies, proposed more punishment for the illegal downloading of films and television shows. Ni Ping defended the use

of dialects in drama, and her arguments were convincing since she has the double roles of TV hostess and actress. And then, there were the proposals typical of bleeding-heart liberals, such as Pu Cunxin's call to ban smoking and Yang Lan's for energy-saving architecture.

More vague than Gong Li's motion was Gong Hanlin's appeal to "raise the aesthetic standard of the nation", which involves more filtering of content. I admire his good intention, but has not he thought about the possible negative fallout?

Not every entertainer-cum-temp politician treats this event with seriousness. Some probably see their presence as window-dressing. For those not politically inclined, the change of status – albeit temporary – could be onerous. Representing the people, even a small number, is serious business. Some are better off sticking to their day jobs, in which they excel. And I do not blame Liu Xiang for his absence. He is contributing much more to his country by competing in international games than, say, asking the government to pay more attention to sports.

NPC deputies and CPPCC members should guard the interests of their professions, but they should not go above national interests. When Ling Jiefang, pen name February River, suggested tax exemption for writers "to stimulate cultural creativity", he was rightly criticized, even by his peers.

The biggest news this year was Zhao Benshan's failure to make the cut as an NPC deputy. The popular comedian is the "pride of Liaoning", but he was voted out at the province level. People are making distinctions between good entertainers and good representatives, and the media should follow suit.

54. Rocker's sad show a lesson to media hounds

May 13, 2006

Would you be surprised by some erratic behavior of a rock 'n' roll star? Obviously, many were caught off guard when news of Dou Wei rampaging through a newsroom became the entertainment story du jour.

On Wednesday afternoon, Dou, a member of a local band, marched into the office of The Beijing News and demanded to meet a reporter who recently wrote about him. According to news reports, Dou Wei smashed a computer, a disk player and some windows. Later, he returned to set fire to a car that was parked outside of the building. The newspaper called the police and Dou was detained.

In Thursday's edition, The Beijing News said that the two articles Dou disputed were both based on interviews with him and people directly involved in the stories.

While rock singers are not known for their rationality, what Dou did was clearly out of line and beyond what is civilly and legally acceptable. He should have demanded an apology or filed a lawsuit if he truly felt he was defamed.

That said, one must admit that, in the larger scheme of entertainer-press relations, Dou Wei has been a victim of China's burgeoning and chaotic entertainment media.

Dou sealed his fate in 1996 when he married pop diva Faye Wong. They divorced three years later, but his name is forever associated with hers. Dou used to be a promising and talented singer in a well-regarded rock band. However, for years, his stardom has been in decline while his ex-wife reigns supreme in the public eye and is the target of relentless paparazzi even though she has not been active in the scene for quite a while.

It is almost a conspiracy that the nation's tabloids have got into the habit of portraying Dou as the failure and the sad contrast to his former wife's glory. Some reports use melodramatic terms like "wife leaving, kid separating" to describe his situation. One could almost see the gloating and the smirking when they mention that Dou pays his other ex-wife 500 yuan (US$63) in monthly alimony and is paid only 200 yuan (US$25) for each gig.

A performer with such limited earning power will never get his name printed in the entertainment pages no matter what publicity stunt he employs. But Dou has pulled off the biggest feat of all and inadvertently became the reluctant Eddie Fisher to Wong's Elizabeth Taylor.

Dou should have learned to ignore the buzzing and rumbling of the gossip mill. Sadly, he is unable to remain aloof of what others say about him. As recently as last April, he was summoning reporters and sitting for interviews, during which he would make outrageous claims about people around him.

One thing is for sure: He is not cut out for life as a celebrity. He speaks his mind, accentuating and exacerbating public perceptions of him, which have been droned in and reinforced by media reports. In other words, he has turned himself into fodder for the ever-expanding celebrity machine.

Maybe there should be a school for celebrities – I don't know whether the Beijing Film Academy has courses on how to feed lines to the press that reflect glowingly on entertainers. People like Dou should receive training on deflecting damaging innuendos and not let a little bad publicity get on their nerves.

It is time that Dou sought psychiatric counseling. And it is also time that the nation's entertainment reporters left alone those who do not want to be exploited by the glaring light.

Chapter Nine
Cherish Our Tradition, Sensibly

55. Appreciate *Guoxue* as it is

June 30, 2007

Guoxue is hot, it is sizzling.

Guoxue is the study of traditional Chinese culture, especially Confucianism. In much of the past century, it was the target of relentless criticism, something to be thrown out, bath water, baby and all. Now, it is dangerously close to being overhyped as the panacea for all social ills.

Just this week, a principal of a painting and calligraphy school in the Central China city of Zhengzhou knelt down in piety while handing out 5,000 free copies of a Confucian booklet that is the equivalent of *Do's and Don'ts for Students*.

In my mind, people like him are not showing respect for our cultural heritage, but making a travesty of it. I understand why people of previous generations went to extreme lengths to trash *Guoxue*. They needed to get rid of its constraints that had bound us for thousands of years. The country was in dire need of an injection of fresh air and new thinking.

In a time of peace and

prosperity like ours, we should not be cynical about *Guoxue*, but appreciate it for all the wealth and beauty of civilization it embodies. Our education should include mandatory teaching of a sampling of the *Guoxue* classics.

But, as they say, a little knowledge is a dangerous thing. Some who are recently exposed to *Guoxue* tend to place it on a pedestal that even normal criticism and academic analysis is seen as heresy. In essence, they want to revert to the old days when *Guoxue* was a force of suppression rather than a source of inspiration.

Many people get their *Guoxue* inklings from such channels as CCTV's *Lecture Room*, where eloquent speakers like Yu Dan offered a chicken-soup-for-the-soul interpretation. There is nothing wrong with this populist methodology, but hers is far from a definitive account. Instead, it is more an appetizer that should lead to a feast of the main entrée, which is the original work with its complexities and subtleties that her feel-good preaching could not possibly incorporate.

This is like claiming that McDonald's and KFC are the greatest American food, or Hollywood is the representative of American culture. This line of reasoning leads to the boom of rebuilding old architecture while the real thing is happily destroyed to make way for more development.

Many want the facade of reverence with the soothing spirituality and regained self-esteem. They are not unlike the proverbial Lord Ye, who prays for a dragon all his life, but when the dragon descends, would flee in panic.

People who revere *Guoxue* as God Almighty do not really understand how civilizations evolve. They believe it is this rigid thing that must be crammed down the throat of youngsters and never accommodate their questions. Most traditional style schools (*si shu*) that have sprung up in recent years resort to this gorging-without-digesting approach.

The turmoil in the past century kept many Chinese untethered from the rich heritage of our culture. Now some would use scraps of it as a paper-weight and a refuge, so that they have a sense of belonging to something great, not something to be pounded by a newer, more aggressive culture. It has become a defense mechanism, so to speak, against uncertainties of the ever-globalizing world.

The purists reject any outside influence, oblivious that many of what they consider authentically Chinese, such as the traditional musical instrument *erhu*, were originally imported. They want to crown the Han-style costume as the national standard, not realizing those who conquered and ruled central China have long been part of the big family of China's multiple ethnicities, therefore their way of dressing just as authentic Chinese as the Han's.

What the *Guoxue* fundamentalists have ignored is something preached by Confucius – understanding and tolerance.

56. Kneeling is a thing of the past

December 30, 2006

How far should job applicants go to show they are keen?

A 38-year-old graduate from Hunan Province resorted to begging – kneeling down before his potential employer.

Now, I know the job market is tough. But what does bending down on your knees and kowtowing achieve other than to humiliate yourself? Nothing. Unless the employer likes that sort of thing. It turned out that President Chen of the Hunan Environment and Biology Vocational Institute, who was conducting the job interview, "felt extremely awkward".

Could it be that the student, who majored in Chinese history, was carrying too much baggage of all things traditionally Chinese? One would think that going down on bended knees, together with foot binding, had been consigned to the rubbish bin of history when the Qing Dynasty collapsed.

Obviously it is still in fashion, kind of. If you flip through the channels and pause at any costume drama, you're bound to catch glimpses of ministers prostrating themselves in front of the emperor, or peasants on all fours in front of anybody who may grant them favor or mercy.

It is sad to see such historical dramatizations spill over into real life in an era when everybody is supposed to be equal and human dignity respected.

Incidents of kneeling crop up in the press from time to time and at the most unusual times or places. A couple of years ago, some hair salons invented a service that made kneeling mandatory for the workers while washing customers' hair. That surely made them very uncomfortable, both physically and psychologically, and it did not really increase the comfort level of the customers unless they took pleasure in debasing other people.

In the early 1990s, when China's nouveaux riche had not yet learnt how to squander their money tastefully, there were reportedly private clubs where all service personnel would pour drinks and light cigarettes while hunkering down. That must have made the patrons feel like emperors sitting on a throne.

Ironically, a few students who demanded that authorities respect their rights and freedom went down on their knees while presenting their plea in a very public place. Could this be black humor? Certainly not to the kneelers.

Maybe, in their minds, one has to stoop low in order to raise oneself a little. Maybe that was the manifestation of the tactical detour, what we Chinese call the "can bend, can stretch" spirit, a metaphor generally involving the arms rather than the legs.

I am not against genuflection per se. At the annual Tomb-Sweeping Day, or before the Spring Festival, I kneel and pray as part of a family ceremony to remember my deceased ancestors. When visiting temples I may also do this in front of the giant Buddha, even though I am not a Buddhist, either practicing or at heart.

For me, to drop to my knees in front of another human being would only mean that the person is dead, which would be an implicit curse, would it not? But that's just my quirk. When a billion bucks falls into my lap, I may think differently and envisage a harem of supermodels all shorter than I am.

There is something ritualistically sadistic or masochistic about all this. It is the most visible sign of subordination. The kneeler forfeits his self-esteem, and the one knelt to gains a sense of superiority. As interpreted by the British governess in *The King and I*, you become a "toad" once you put yourself so low that your forehead touches the ground.

However, kneeling is symbolic. If you remove all the status connotations, it causes a little discomfort to the kneeler and brings nothing concrete to the one sitting or standing. Which means if you have a knack for acting, you don't lose anything when impersonating a "toad."

This has led me to think that there must be at least two kinds of kneelers – real self-debasers who would do anything short of cutting off a limb, and pretenders who just want to boost the ego of the other party. The salon girls who do this for a living must have accepted it as play-acting or a way to earn tips. Otherwise, they would be miserable.

For those who get satisfaction out of being knelt to, the joy of seeing someone artificially crouch down could make up for their insecurities. But they should realize that when they make another person lower in stature, they make themselves even lower in respectability.

57. Kowtowing not best show of gratitude

January 27, 2007

Winter vacation is around the corner, and a management school at Zhengzhou University has given one special assignment to students happily going home to celebrate Spring Festival: kowtow to their parents.

The students are generally not pleased, according to media reports. The school explained that kowtowing is the highest manifestation of gratitude in China, and to do that to your parents during the Chinese New Year is not asking too much.

I don't know what's in the students' minds, but I don't think it's a good idea, either. Now I have to engage in some fancy footwork to avoid self-contradiction because I had previously supported a similar task: washing your parents' feet.

In a fast-urbanizing world where human interaction becomes increasingly superficial, it is important to reinforce the fragile ties between parents and their children, who tend to drift away both physically and psychologically. The school authority is right to remind students that reviewing textbooks,

Father and mother, please accept my kowtow!

partying and food binges are not the be-all and end-all when it comes to the holiday. There is one virtue that should never be neglected in any modern society – love for your parents.

And it deserves to be on the educational agenda. Given the "little emperor" status of most children in China, appreciation is something that should indeed be hammered home once in a while to replace the natural sense of entitlement.

However, kowtowing is awkward. It implies supplication and is more often associated, through endless images in television soap operas, with inferiority. It is more a symbol of submission and respect than one of love and thankfulness.

I'm not against children who willingly kowtow to their folks. Physically it is by no means acrobatic, but if forced to perform the act, people will adjust their mentality and strip the gesture of any inherent meaning, which will evolve into another vacuous ritual.

Just imagine a kid who kneels and knocks his head on the floor to his parents on every possible occasion, and then turns around to take drugs and gambles away the family fortune. Would the kowtowing lessen their parents' heartbreak?

Washing feet could also degenerate into an inane ritual if the school rigidly enforces such an assignment. But it has obvious advantages over kowtowing: It is less symbolic; and since it involves physical contact, it could have an electrifying effect when it's first performed. I've heard that some children and parents experience a magic moment of bonding during the process.

Honestly, I cannot imagine kowtowing will have the same impact. Most probably, the parent will laugh a little out of unease and say "Arise! Arise!" which is a common line in costume drama. Every-one will regard it as play-acting, just like the offering and refusal of cigarettes as a greeting routine.

No, I don't think it is humiliating to kowtow to mom and dad if, unlike in feudal dynasties, it does not entail the surrender of one's free will. But as a token of love, it is just not as heartfelt and pragmatic as other options.

Here are some alternatives:

You can attend one less gathering with old buddies and instead scrub the floor, wash the dishes and do the laundry. In that way, your parents can enjoy a well-deserved rest.

Or you can take your parents for a walk in the local park, chatting with their buddies for a change. That'll probably take up a few hours of "Nintendo time".

In the very least, you can hug your parents and say: "Thank you for your love." Why give "free hugs" to strangers on the street when you can give it to the people who deserve it most?

58. Is the dragon too fearsome a symbol for China?

December 09, 2006

When Guangming Daily interviewed Wu Youfu, the Party secretary of the Shanghai International Studies University talked at great length about the implicit hazards of having the dragon as China's national symbol. However, when the tabloids picked up the story, it turned into headlines like "Some scholars suggest retiring the dragon", with more than a whiff of discontent in the tone. The underlying message was: How dare you suggest something so abominable as to forsake our ancestry?

This was not the first time I've seen market-driven newspapers disguising commentaries as news reports. Evoking unpatriotic implications is the surest way to enhance one's own image of moral correctness and at the same time sell papers. But it pollutes the air of free and open discourse.

Why can't someone versed in cross-cultural references point out the disparate understandings of a special image that carries layers of meaning throughout our

civilization?

Remember the days when China made a toothpaste called "Fangfang" and tried to sell it overseas? Someone like Professor Wu could have come along and told them that no English-speaking consumer would buy a product that might turn their teeth into fangs.

A symbol like the dragon exists for two purposes: To exemplify our collective traits, and to help other people understand us. If what they may perceive differs from what we want to project, the symbol would have failed on at least one of these counts. Professor Wu was not putting down centuries-old Chinese heritage, but making it relevant in the age of globalization, when China is rising fast on the world stage and cares a lot about how it is seen by others.

That said, I don't support his proposal. And like Wu, I'm approaching it from a technical rather than emotional point of view.

The usefulness of the mythical beast outlasts any potential drawback. In essence, the dragon is like a school mascot. The difference is that since it carries the history of thousands of years and represents a fifth of the world's population, tinkering is impractical.

Given the circumstances, it would be more practicable to reshape perception rather than the image itself. True, when Westerners conjure up the idea of the dragon, it's likely to be a fiery beast of destruction. But don't forget, when we Chinese think of a mouse, it is an annoying creature that nibbles our food and spreads disease. Walt Disney single-handedly transformed it into a cute character that can sing and dance to our delight.

Changes are already on the way. In countries like the United States, dragon boat racing and the dragon dance are making inroads from Chinatown into the mainstream. From my observation, not even kids are scared.

The dragon in the West does not invoke the same fearful reaction as a carnivorous dinosaur, but rather a feeling of awe. It is not as awe-inspiring as the dinosaur, granted, and certainly not as beloved as the panda.

The real problem, as I see it, is the dragon's close association with imperial power, which is reinforced every night through TV soap operas. When we watch people who are willing to kill millions for access to the "dragon seat", it instills something into the psyche of our children, something incongruous with the growth of our nation.

So, the first step for the image overhaul is to take the dragon down from its throne and make it a little more egalitarian.

59. Be sincere in preservation of cultural artifacts

September 02, 2006

What is the use of a house if you don't have the money to maintain it and it's probably doomed to destruction? Well, by selling it to someone who plans to move it to Europe, you can raise public awareness to such an extent that local officials put it on the endangered list. This was what happened in July when an old house in Anhui Province suddenly got elevated to the status of "cultural relic".

"Green Screen Abode" is a 200-year-old teahouse that has fallen into disrepair. "We had to sell it because we have no means to keep it in working condition. But once it is outside China, it'll be protected as a museum for tea," said the original owner. The new buyer, a corporate executive, planned to move the house to Sweden piece by piece, then reassemble it and restore it to its former splendor.

But that was before the building got special attention.

For me, the whole story is ironic: If a foreign relocation scheme had not surfaced, this house would most probably have crumbled like many others in similar situations. As a local official put it, "We're a poor county. We don't have the financial resources to protect the designated relics, let alone private properties scattered here and there."

Even in the nation's capital, whole stretches of the traditional *hutong* are being razed to make way for so-called "modern" buildings. Countless complaints and protests have been launched, but to no avail. Where are the preservation-minded officials

when you need them?

It seems that when purchase by a foreign party is involved, our national psyche can be easily bruised. To use an oft-quoted refrain, that would be like "selling a national treasure cheap". But the secret to public aversion towards foreign ownership of things old lies in our embedded sense of history. In the old days when China's door was forced open by Western power, our ancestors did not have the means or even the sense to protect our own heritage. Ancient architectures were pillaged and plundered, and artifacts looted.

But we must realize that things have changed. Now we have laws and regulations designed to preserve and protect, albeit not implemented to everyone's satisfaction. We should overcome the victim mentality when dealing with foreign parties on loans, purchases or relocation of cultural relics. Those who abide by Chinese laws should not be treated with discrimination. Whoever takes the trouble and expense to move an old house overseas for reassembling surely cherishes the architecture.

As a matter of fact, when it comes to illegal acts of vandalism, such as cutting off a Buddha's head and smuggling it across the border, it is greed and wanton disregard for laws and decency that are at work, by crooked Chinese and foreign nationals alike.

There is a fundamental difference between someone who bribes a local to steal a piece of an artifact and someone who legally buys something of cultural value and exports it. The role of the government is to spell out what can and cannot be bought for overseas destinations and to guard those irreplaceable items that are an integral part of our cultural inheritance.

I'm not implying the Anhui house should be allowed to be moved to Sweden. I believe our existing laws probably have made it quite clear. But if it is within the realm of protection, local authorities should not have waited until it got into the headlines before they took action.

My point is, if there is no option for protection by ourselves, I'd rather see it re-erected in Sweden and used an exemplar of Chinese culture than see it fall into decay in its homeland.

Two decades ago, I accompanied a few curators from China on a tour of the San Francisco Asian Art Museum. While walking through the properly air-conditioned and ventilated vault, one of them sighed: "In our museum, this kind of stuff just lies in the backyard with no shelter from rain or wind."

Psychologically, this is not a unique issue for China. In the animated film *Toy Story 2*, Woody the toy cowboy falls out of favor with his owner. But a museum in Japan wants to display him and other quintessentially American toys to Japanese kids. Woody resisted the idea of moving at first, but then embraced the prospect of new popularity and possible immortality in a foreign museum.

My conjecture is, if a Chinese government agency had paid for the Anhui house and designated it as an exhibit for Chinese civilization in Sweden, there might have been no controversy.

60. No need to standardize a saint's look

I can safely bet that, of the billions of people in the world today, nobody has seen Confucius in person. I can also bet you everything I have that nobody has seen a photograph of him, either.

You see, Confucius was born in 551 B. C., well before photography came into existence. Yet, some organization wants to standardize his portrait to "give him a single, recognizable identity around the world".

The China Confucius Foundation will create this visual rendering "with advice from Confucian scholars, historians, artists and his descendants", and unveil it during the September celebration of his 2,557th birthday.

I never knew for 2000-plus years that I should look like this.

Confucius

Standard look of Confucius

None of them has seen Confucius or his likeness except the earliest painting of him by Wu Daozi of the Tang Dynasty (618-907 AD), on which the standard portrait will reportedly be based. But Wu and Confucius lived more than 1,000 years apart. His painting at best incorporated written descriptions from an earlier time, or was most likely a work of his own imagination.

The disturbing thing is not that the foundation wants to issue a portrait that it touts as "standard", but that it wants to stamp out all other images of the Great Sage because it claims they "will severely harm his good aura and personal charisma and will hinder the propagation of his thoughts".

So, how will our benchmark Confucius look? He will be an old man with a long beard, broad mouth and big ears. He will wear a robe and cross his hands on his chest.

Was Confucius never a boy who enjoyed mischief, a young man who frolicked, a curmudgeon who resisted new ideas, an old man who got lonely? He might have gone through those times and moods like everyone else, but if the foundation has its way, he will now be forever embalmed in one particular portrayal. No variations and creativity allowed.

The problem is not whether the "standard portrait" will be authentic – it does reflect the Confucius in most people's minds – but whether interpretations will benefit or harm his stature, and by extension, the fabric of our society. Therefore, it does not matter whether portraits from the Spring and Autumn and Warring States Periods exist or what kind of organization the China Confucius Foundation is.

There is simply no need to standardize such a thing as the image of Confucius.

There are certain things in a civilized society that should be standardized. For example, laws and regulations, and most obviously, measurements. But do we need uniformity when it comes to how people react to a movie or a book, and in this case, a portrayal? There were times in our history when liking one movie or hating another was identified as "incorrect", as in "politically incorrect". The giant steamroller of conformity would crush any trace of individuality and pulverize it into dust under a paved road.

Now that we realize how ludicrous it was to make everyone feel the same way about something so personal, we may also laugh at the futility and folly of regulating Confucius' visual depiction. Even if the foundation's claim had validity, it would be impossible to enforce it beyond the border. Are they going to tear down the Confucius statue in New York's Chinatown if it does not fit their profile?

The real danger behind the portrait homogenizing scheme is the effort to control how we see Confucius and Confucianism. Thirty years ago, we were force-fed the notion that he represented all the evils of Chinese culture; and now, we are supposed to kneel down and kowtow.

While I believe every Chinese student should study some Confucianism, we should steer clear of the pitfall of blind idolatry. Yes, a lot of his teachings are relevant today, but some are evidently out of date, such as blind obedience to the authorities and father figures and contempt for women.

The important thing is, everyone should have the right to approach Confucianism with independent thinking and critique his theories without the coercion of standard answers.

That is not the same as being disrespectful. If there is one Chinese who should be enshrined, it is probably Confucius. But treating him as an icon of Chinese civilization does not preclude that we read him with our own opinions or portray him from our individual minds' eyes.

Diversity in interpretation will only make Confucianism stronger, not more confusing.

61. A memorial service, outsourced

April 08, 2006

April 5th was Qingming Festival, or Tomb-Sweeping Day, when people pay homage to their deceased family members. The ideal weather for this day, as sanctified in an ancient poem, is a drizzle, which would on one hand compliment the solemnity of the occasion and on the other hand eliminate fire hazards.

The latest addition to this custom is a paid service that lets others, presumably professionals, take care of all the incense burning and tomb sweeping for you. The fee is not unreasonable – about 200-300 yuan (US$25-38) – and as seen on TV news, a group of four people, properly dressed in dark suits, pray in front of a designated tombstone, and in case you fear a scam, videotape the whole process and e-mail it to the client.

Everything seems to be prim and proper, except that there is no sense in the whole thing. Sending a stranger to meditate at a tombstone is fundamentally different from sending a nurse to take care of an ailing parent. In the first case, lighting up candles and placing flowers are outward manifestations of one's remembrance of a loved one who is no longer with them. The gestures are all symbolic.

If one is unable to make the trip to the site, it doesn't mean one misses his or her dear departed any less. Asking a relative or a close friend to go in your stead makes sense, but asking a total stranger is a little preposterous.

It's somewhat like attending a church service: If you're religious, you may go or not go, depending on your time schedule and a thousand other things that prompt or prevent you from attending. But it would be hypocritical to hire someone to go in your name, wouldn't it? It's your soul that's at stake, after all.

The incident reported in the news happened in Shanghai, like all new and newsworthy business models, is quickly being copied in other cities.

Is it a sign of commercialization running amok? We are so busy making money that we'll hire professionals to do the memorial ritual for us. What's next? Shall we hire help to go on a date for us? They'll surely be more eloquent and charming than we are because they'll be selected from a large pool of talented and trained individuals.

Others might argue that some people live far away from where their ancestors are buried, and feel the deceased in the other world would know and be sad if nobody showed up at their tombstones. Well, if their spirits were alive, how would they feel when they see total strangers come for visit? It wouldn't be better than when we open our doors and find salespeople.

That reminds me of the story of college students "renting" girlfriends on their winter trips home. Equally ludicrous at first glance, this practice smells fishy and may involve intentions far more down-to-earth than something as spiritual as communicating one's sense of love and loss.

Vanity, an urge to please the parents, and convenience to secure a temporary sex partner could be possible factors.

It is a good thing that all kinds of services are created to cater to the needs of a rapidly evolving society. This way, jobs multiply and wealth spreads. The benefits of a free market trickle, albeit slowly, to all corners of the society.

However, there are things so personal that no assistant or machine, no matter how scientifically trained or programmed, can substitute. "Tomb sweeping", the Chinese term for the ceremony, is one.

That said, I have to admit that part of the service can indeed be outsourced – the physical part, the part about removing weeds and cleaning up the tomb. But shouldn't that have been the job of the cemetery?

When most people talk about "sweeping their ancestral tombs", it is metaphorical as well as literal. Money can buy flowers, candles and incense, but money cannot buy the remembrance one has for the lamented.

62. Yes, Spring Festival is truly golden

February 16, 2007

When it comes to Spring Festival, many Chinese have similar memories and ideas: How joyous it was when we were kids, how routine and stale it has become, and how much it is threatened by the more exotic Western holidays now making inroads in China.

For one, I wouldn't trade anything for Spring Festival. It is by far the most important holiday and no amount of Westernization will change that. Yes, we're less likely to jump up and down in jubilation now that we are grownups, but we should not be cynical about it either.

When I was a kid, lunar New Year was a big thing because we could enjoy 12-course feasts for days and were given new clothes and red envelopes by parents and grandparents. In a time when everything was rationed, just imagine what a thrill the occasion would be.

Nowadays, it is difficult to recreate that feeling, even for kids. We can eat like that every day. (Well, actually, the trend is to eat less and eat healthy.) And we can afford new clothes whenever we want, at least for the growing middle class. But even for those at the lower strata of society,

material life has improved so much that an ordinary day today resembles this holiday a generation ago.

So, what still makes it special? In a small measure, firecrackers.

I'm not superstitious and don't care much about driving devils away and other such folklore. But having a panorama of fireworks when the clock strikes midnight on New Year's Eve is one experience that sets my heart palpitating and sends me into a holiday mood faster than anything else – and I'm not even crazy about sparklers.

Now, firecrackers have safety hazards. But to ban them on these grounds is just like banning all vehicles because traffic fatalities in an entire country amount to the number of casualties in a war. I guess firefighters have to work overtime during this season and people still need to take precautions, but it is a small price to pay for the atmosphere of festivity.

The centerpiece, of course, is the family reunion. Spending this time away from home is, to say the least, miserable. That's why people take a sizable chunk of their annual income to trek home and do things they do year after year, such as buying gifts for loved ones, drinking with old buddies and indulging in all-night reminiscences.

It is a ritual that binds us together as one culture. It may not be economically optimum, but a lot of our traditions don't really make economic sense. We can revise the other two golden weeks to reduce their strains on resources, but the New Year holiday is one golden week that cannot be adjusted. No matter how you spend the time, you want it to be joyous and fruitful, something to make a year of hard work worthwhile.

Lunar New Year, for all its pagan origin, reminds me of Christmas. It is essentially about loving, giving and sharing. I was taught that, even if you are the most disgusting miser or snob, you should not turn away a beggar during this time, but should instead feed him what you have. In other words, if you want to be blessed, you should spread your bliss.

Last year, I interviewed a woman who has a small business in Beijing. On New Year's Day she took her daughter to visit not a relative but an old lady with no children. They brought her gifts and cooked a traditional meal for her.

"It's just a small thing I can do to make her less lonely," she said, asking me not to reveal her real name or make a big deal out of it.

This random act of kindness to a stranger may not be on the traditional holiday agenda, but that makes the Spring Festival spirit all the more heartwarming.

63. *Chunyun* provides a glimpse of China's reality

February 02, 2008

Eleven years ago, I took a train from Shanghai to Beijing during the Spring Festival rush, known as *chunyun*. I got a ticket in a hard-seat car as no other seats were available. As a result, I was squeezed into a space so small I could not turn left or right. And forget about going to the restroom; it was occupied by as many as eight passengers. During the 24-hour journey, I did not eat or drink anything – just to avoid going to the toilet.

It was a trip to remember. Anyone who wants to understand China – of ordinary Chinese, not just those frequenting five-star hotels – should get on a hard-seat train during *chunyun*, at least once. For one thing, you will instantly realize why China has a family planning policy.

I should add that my journey was not interrupted by snowstorms or delays. So, I can imagine what those millions of home-bound people stranded in trains, buses and railway stations are going through, both physically and mentally. After days of waiting at the Guangzhou Railway Station, reported Southern

Metropolis News, passengers were finally allowed to board trains. However, they did not burst into joy, but tears.

Even without the complications of bad weather, *chunyun* is a harrowing experience. The Lunar New Year is part of a tradition that makes us who we are as Chinese. Just as Chinese characters (logograms) are not ideal for computer input, this most important of Chinese holidays puts an incredible strain on the nation's transport network.

I am sure when our ancestors sat around a fire with the whole family they had no idea what chaos family reunions could cause. Likewise, when Cangjie invented Chinese characters 4,600 years ago, he could not have foreseen the era of typewriters and computers. However, that is not a reason why we should simplify things by getting rid of those elements our current infrastructure or technology cannot accommodate. Science and technology exist to help us keep our heritage, not to reduce us to an economically optimum existence that has no richness.

That does not mean I am in favor of everybody making the journey home regardless of circumstances. On the contrary, each person should weigh the costs when making a decision. And this year, the odds are stacked against the customary "I'll be home for the New Year".

When I was a kid – a time of shortages, this holiday meant new clothes and enough food for several days. Now, most Chinese can live every day as if it is the Spring Festival, and we realize it is not just the material things that make us long for the season, it is the warmth of sitting around a big table with family members and relatives – your parents whom you have not seen for 12 months, your aunt who doted on you when you were a toddler, and even your high-school friend.

As our family structure keeps shrinking, we will probably see in our lifetime the disappearance of big families, and we will recall with fond memories the good old days when family members journeyed distances – some even from abroad – to share New Year's Eve watching a television show and feasting.

Spring Festival is a big money-spinner for many businesses, but for those who take days off to spend with their families it has nothing to do with economics. Yes, we give red envelopes, but they only add to the joy of the festival. I wish everyone, especially those who have been through the snowstorms, happiness in the coming year.

Chapter Ten
Language Matters

64. Hyperbole in advertising

April 02, 2007

Recently, not a week has gone by without the national television station uncovering another case of advertising fraud: Two weeks ago, it was some kind of tea that claimed to be a secret Tibetan concoction with weight-loss potency. This week, a wok advertised as non-sticky and non-smoky was found to be just a regular cooking utensil with none of the purported functions.

I wonder why people take delight in such exposés. If product safety officials had done their job, reporters with little knowledge of product technicality would not have these scoops. Unlike last year's flurry of cases, this year's were meant to rob – not to kill – you. When I talk to some entrepreneurs – not in the capacity of a reporter, of course, I often get the refrain that it's okay to exaggerate the power of your product as long as it does not poison the consumer.

This is their ethical bottom-line. It is a great leap forward from those that would do anything for a buck. As one woman who splurged a few hundred yuan on the "Tibetan tea"

complained to China Central Television (CCTV), "the money was nothing, but I thought I could shed a few pounds and I was swindled!" It was the psychological damage rather than monetary loss that gave her grief.

In a sense, consumers like her had it coming. Chinese people have always had a penchant for elixirs that can cure everything. In the old days when quacks sold their potions at flea markets, they literally put up notices that emphasized the "one hundred illnesses" they could heal. When I was a kid, I would tease them by naming strange symptoms they failed to include on the list. They would shoot back: "Sure, this herb is the best for that! Didn't I tell you it's guaranteed to treat a hundred diseases? A hundred in Chinese means every one. You dummy!"

We are brought up in a culture of hyperbole. We used to shout the emperor would live ten thousand years, even though it was inflated a hundred times for the best possible scenario of current life expectancy. But nobody seemed to mind.

Likewise, we pick similarly florid words for denunciation. Saying someone "deserves a thousand stabs and ten thousand cuts" may sound like a grueling scene from a horror flick, but it's no more emphatic than "deserving to die", sometimes even in taunting. I remember a Chinese student in New York had a spat with his friend and hurled words to this effect. He was arrested and charged with attempted murder when the police got a verbatim translation of his threat.

Such figures of speech permeate our lives. In school, we were promised a beautiful world where everything we ever needed would magically fall into our lap. It was not called "utopia". Maybe kids, or the kid in us, need these kinds of soothing fairy tales to transport us into a fantasyland of perfect harmony.

The course of growing up is, in a way, the process of learning to strip away the pretensions from the essence. Nowadays, cynics begin to turn the clichés on their heads. For example, "famous" is so overused that anyone with a whiff of name or position would crown himself a "famous" something. Along came comedian Guo Degang, who labeled himself "non-famous" and became an overnight sensation.

Then, Guo, like other celebrities, went into overdrive to cash in on his popularity. For a reported two million yuan, he appeared in ad campaigns for the above-mentioned brand of "Tibetan tea"; but he tried to maintain his "otherness" by refusing to appear on the CCTV Spring Festival gala, an over-blown show with caricatured expressions of joy.

Suffice it to say, it's not easy to be nimble in the midst of landmines of fancy words and trite metaphors.

65. Hyperbole in advertising: redux

May 19, 2007

In a recent discussion on the supervision of outdoor advertising, Beijing Mayor Wang Qishan remarked that the repeated use of certain words on real estate billboards has marred the image of the capital city. These words include "luxury", "ultimate", "deluxe", "exclusive", etc. They all suggest the lifestyle of the super rich.

Obviously the huddled masses cannot afford these properties. As a matter of fact, calculated by average income, even a not-so-luxury apartment is out of the reach of most residents. For example, a 50-square-meter unit, priced at 10,000 yuan per square meter, will take 8.3 years for a person who earns 5,000 yuan a month.

If you dissect the political jargon, these adverts upset ordinary people. The poor may already be numb, or they would have been driven crazy. The segment of society that is really distressed may be the middle class, including young professionals, who see themselves as economically enslaved for a lifetime to real estate developers.

The issue is not simply a poor ver-

sus rich dichotomy. From the perspective of freedom of expression, I don't think advertising slogans should be regulated. They are designed to hook, stimulate, and provoke. If ad copy, especially the tagline, reads like a government document, the ad agency would probably be fired.

Ad slogans have frequently been criticized as damaging linguistic purity. They twist idioms and proverbs. They coin new words that are not yet enshrined in the dictionary. They make puns that are too titillating for some to accept.

However, they have done a good job reaching their target audience. Housing ads that flaunt wealth and status reflect – as much as steer – customer mentality. Many properties adopt foreign names, such as Yosemite and Napa Valley, because people tend to associate such Western style with top quality and privilege.

In the 1990s, a southern city outlawed the use of "president" and "imperial" in property names. That did not dent the craving for showing off wealth. Banning the current batch of ostentatious adjectives would not achieve the desired effect either. If anything, a new regulation of this nature may only make the advertisers less reliant on clichés and make them more imaginative in terms of how they express themselves.

Basically this is a question of taste. In a mature society displaying wealth is generally considered bad taste. But for those who have just shaken off the shackles of poverty, there is a constant need for reaffirmation as if one wakes up from a bad dream and does not stop biting his fingers.

Even in the United States, such flaunting still exists, though more subtly. Real estate ads use generic terms such as "top-quality" and "spacious" to attract the lower-income crowd and more specific descriptions such as "granite" and "gated" to denote higher class. One needs a sharp-eyed agent to wade through the warm and fuzzy façade and get to their true meaning.

What makes China's housing adjectives such a pain in the neck are housing prices, not the over-the-top, kitschy exaggerations, which are common in most realms of Chinese expression. Yet, government policies rarely alleviate that woe.

Let's imagine that all these real estate ads are replaced with ads for arts and antiques. They also cater to the super rich. Yet they would not elicit the same response from drivers and pedestrians. The reason is simple: arts and antiques are not essentials in our lives. The rich can play the wealth accumulation game without affecting the living standards of the masses.

But when housing is played like a card game, wide swaths of our society are affected. The pompous ad slogans only become the frost on top of the snow, so to speak, aggravating the sinking and frozen feeling.

66. Platitude overload depreciates language

April 01, 2006

Language clarifies, but when used rigidly, it often conceals and confounds.

A street slogan in a northeastern city has sparked a debate, proving that public mentality is so entrenched on linguistic matters that even a little toying is met with a wall of frowns.

The slogan that recently appeared in Shenyang of Liaoning Province is intended to discourage

unlicensed drivers. Under normal circumstances, one might see a call such as "Severely punish unlicensed driving," or some variation of it. The poster in question borrowed a line from the popular movie *A World Without Thieves* and twisted it into, "I detest unlicensed driving because it does not have any technical difficulty in it."

Some people just don't have a sense of humor. They have dissected the "technical difficulty" part without understanding that the catchphrase has a life of its own ever since the movie premiered more than a year ago.

That's the biggest strength of Feng Xiaogang's films, which are always able to create simple but memorable lines that eventually work into everyday

conversations.

But for the most part, we live in a world of clichés.

If you read a Chinese newspaper, there are word combinations that are more inseparable than conjoined twins. Look no further than "warmly welcome" or "actively participate".

Is there such a thing as a lukewarm welcome? If there is, it doesn't seem to exist in China. From what I've experienced, "warmly welcome" usually refers to a reception that is ceremonious and utterly lacking in spontaneity or warmth. It would be more accurate to use "routinely welcome" instead.

"Study hard" is the literal translation of another Chinese banality that has dogged us for decades. How hard counts as "hard"? Reading 400 pages a day? In the ancient times, we had expressive descriptions such as the one for the student who hanged his hair around a girder so he wouldn't doze off while poring over Confucius. That is how vivacious the Chinese language used to be.

When words are used indiscriminately or simply overused, they lose their vitality. I remember in the 1970s every store in China had a maxim of top-10 things to adhere to and it always included, "Be nice to customers." But in that age of scarcity, sales people wore a customary look of disdain on their faces. There was not even a hint of contrast or black humor. The to-do words on the poster had been sapped of their dictionary-sanctioned meanings.

Nothing dulls a language faster than an overload of platitudes. There are many culprits: Bureaucrats who stick to a small set of officialese and hammer it into public sub-consciousness, business executives who pick up fancy terms from MBA programs and couch a plain "You're fired" in resource management jargon, and scholars who insist on rejecting new coinages because they were created by teenagers.

The same is true everywhere. I once was enamored with US presidential speeches. Penned by writers like Peggy Noonon, they seemed to be fresh and devoid of triteness.

Then I noticed the words "hero" and "coward". American politicians have a penchant to call victims "heroes". If you are caught by the enemy and beaten up, you are hailed as a "hero", and if you blow up a building and kill yourself and 1,000 innocent people, you are a "coward".

I wonder who first used "coward" in this context. Is it because your enemy would call him a "hero" so you'd have to use the antonym? A "suicide killer" might be a "merciless desperado" but he is definitely not weak or faint-hearted, which are synonymous with cowardly. I believe the first user of "hero" or "coward" in this sense was a genius. He bent the dictionary definition and achieved rhetorical effect. Then the US presidents imitated him, creating a semantic paradox.

The writer of the Shenyang poster instinctively knew that "severely punish" would be as good as invisible. So, he opted for an "it" phrase. If anything, he was not innovative enough. He should have invented his own axiom, and then he'll become a linguistic hero.

67. Cutting out the waffle in speeches

January 26, 2008

At a recent meeting in Chongqing municipality, deputy mayor Huang Qifan cut short a lower official who was reading from a prepared document: "There's no need to use these bureaucratic clichés on this occasion. It's totally unnecessary." After that, the others skipped at least half of their speeches.

I wish I had the good fortune to be a witness to such a dramatic moment. It was tense, reported a local newspaper, as all those officials who were to report to Huang must have gone through a lightning-fast process to readjust their speaking style – to be concise and to the point.

It would be great if the whole bureaucracy in the nation could be infused with a strong incentive to "cut the waffle".

Officialese is by no means a patently Chinese phenomenon, but it may be more serious here. As far as I know, there is no law or regulation stipulating that an official has to use a jargon-rich, stilted language. However, catchy phrases appearing in official discourse quickly deteriorate into banality.

I am sure there are officials with personal and colorful speech patterns,

but they do not often get broadcast to the masses. Gradually, people assume that you would have to speak in a certain way – usually pompous – to be an official. I bet if CCTV showed a senior office-holder using humor and original figures of speech, it would push the Chinese language into a whole new arena of dynamism.

I guess there are occasions you have to couch your real meaning under layers of verbal blankets, for example, a diplomatic meeting. Then, your audience is equally trained to receive your message and will be able to strip away the layers immediately when deciphering what you mean.

As for ordinary people, they will be so overwhelmed by the tons of clichés that they may be left more perplexed than enlightened. For a newspaper reporter, it is frustrating to sit through hours of prattle just to get to the gist of a speech; and for a television reporter, catching a usable soundbite is just as hard as locating a media darling.

Many bureaucrats are addicted to jargon-laden texts to the point they mistake reading for speaking. A decade ago, I was consulting for a tourism bureau in southern China and asked to prepare a PowerPoint presentation for the boss. Instead of a few pointers, much of his speech was crammed onto the slides – against my advice. The speaker suffered more than I did – he was essentially turned into an elementary school kid who was tested for his ability for memorization the moment he looked away from the screen.

That brings us to the next point: officials should be encouraged to use their own language, and in doing so, have leeway for errors. During a local congress meeting in Wuhan, Party secretary Chen Xunqiu encouraged officials to "speak the truth" and to "omit ceremonial words and cut to the point". To facilitate this, he suggested television reporters turn off their cameras so that people would not worry about saying "the wrong things".

This may not be the ideal way, but currently it is practical. If it is constantly on the minds of speakers not to veer from the official jargon, their hands are tied, which will further restrict their ability to find creative solutions to unique problems. Of course, that deprives us of the positive role models who match their decisive actions with verbal fireworks.

68. Taking pride in our accents

November 19, 2005

There is a tug of war for the stature of dialects in China. On one hand, some government agencies are issuing edicts as God throws thunderbolts, banning the use of dialects on various occasions: No children's programs on television should include dialects; foreign films must not be dubbed into local patois; and television hosts with even the slightest hint of an accent may have to walk.

On the other hand, a groundswell of grassroots activities have set out to defend the rights of using dialects: Blockbuster films like *A World Without Thieves* regularly resort to dialects to ramp up local flavor; radio stations in Sichuan rake in most of their advertising revenues from vernacular shows; and intellectuals join a chorus that preaches the virtues of dialects as the Chinese language's unique strength in its battle against erosion from English.

I believe both approaches are misguided.

Take the purists first. There is nothing wrong with advocating *putonghua*, or Mandarin as it's known in the West, as China's standard speaking lingua franca. But that doesn't mean we should get rid of our local variants.

To enforce a strict "no accent" policy for such public personages as television hosts is not only unnecessary, but also pyrrhic. For example, it has been reported that some of CCTV's most popular hosts did not pass their *putonghua* tests, a prerequisite for their jobs. So what? Peter Jennings, one of the top three anchormen in the United States in the past two decades, had a faint Canadian accent,

though imperceptible to non-native speakers.

Purists seem to be unaware of the benefits and resilience of China's spoken language in its endless mutations. None of the first-generation leaders of New China spoke good *putonghua*, but that added to their charisma and personalities. That's why filmmakers stick to dialects when portraying them on screen.

Producers at CCTV, at the forefront of the linguistic battle, employ Northeastern colloquialisms in their entertainment shows so frequently that the audience in southern parts of the country often feel alienated. Besides, most celebrities are based in Beijing and routinely treat Beijing dialect as if it were *putonghua*. It may be too strong to call them "hypocritical", but it proves that you cannot eliminate local speeches even if you want to.

A dialect can add sparkle to a piece of literature or artwork, and it gives an identity and together-ness to those who share it. However, it keeps away those who don't speak it, or worse, even can't understand it. Unlike the English-speaking world, China has an infinite number of dialects. Where I grew up, as you ride the bike for half an hour passing different villages, pronouns like "we", "you" and "they" start to change. Almost every cluster of villages has a different set for most common words.

The frustration a northerner faces in Guangdong or Shanghai is very real. Language is made for communication, and dialects effectively keep it within a defined circle, for instance, those who are born (or grow up) in a specified geographical location. Anyone who doesn't belong to it instantly turns into an outsider.

Dialects did not spring up by design. It is the result of an inadequacy in transportation (highways), telecommunication (telephones), and mass communication (television). Now that these root causes are collapsing, it is unlikely that young people will make an effort to maintain their linguistic identities based on location alone.

When children from different villages and towns attend the same school, they would not bring their home variations of "we" and "they" with them, but use the ones most dominant in the area, usually the biggest town. When people from across China moved to Shenzhen, it was *putonghua* that they adopted when talking with each another.

Human movements tend to increase with the economy, and most of the small dialects will wither, vanish or be consolidated into regional dialects. But major branches such as Sichuanese, Shanghainese or Cantonese would face no danger at all for the simple reason that the number of speakers for each is so great that no decrees can wipe them out.

Dialects are like living organisms. They go by the law of the survival of the fittest. You can launch wars to suppress them or defend them, but it's the natural laws that are at work here. As long as people communicate, they want to be understood. They will pick up words and descriptions from each other and enrich their own expressions. A term deemed too dialectal today may be accepted usage for all people tomorrow. All we need is to keep an open mind.

69. Variety in name not a bad thing

March 29, 2008

What's in a name? More specifically, what's in the spelling of a place name? Should the Chinese capital be spelt Beijing or Peking?

In a survey jointly conducted by China Youth Daily and Sina.com, a vast majority – 81 percent – opposed the old spelling, with only 10.7 percent supporting it and the rest not caring one way or the other. Opponents of "Peking" hold the view that Chinese proper names should be spelt with the standard *pinyin*. They further elaborate that pandering to the old spelling demonstrates a lack of cultural confidence and subservience to the Western mindset.

For me, this argument reflects the simplistic thinking of some people, especially the young, who habitually flaunt their political correctness. Cultural matters do not fall simply into right or wrong. It is often a tradeoff between two equally flawed choices.

Peking was a Wade-Giles spelling, says one scholar, which was formalized in 1906 by the Imperial Postal Joint-Session Conference; and

the *pinyin* system, which converts it to Beijing, was formally accepted by the UN in 1979.

Love it or hate it, the old form has accumulated so much baggage that you cannot change everything in one fell swoop. For example, the standard name for China's national opera is still Peking Opera. Why not change it to Beijing Opera? I guess Peking Opera was already known throughout the world when the city itself took on the new spelling. Ditto for Peking roast duck and Peking University.

A place name is not like a chemical element. It has more functions than simply denoting a place. It has associations. Great writers may have written about it; great singers sung about it. When you adopt a new name or change the spelling, some of that association will inevitably be lost. Just imagine a company that has spent tens of billions to promote its brand, and then forgo that brand name for something else.

That said, I'm not in favor of changing Beijing back to Peking – for two reasons: Beijing is perfectly pronounceable in English and many other languages; also, Beijing has been in use for three decades and a return to the old spelling would cause more confusion.

However, I strongly support the idea that Guangzhou promotes the old spelling Canton. Unlike Beijing, Guangzhou is not exactly a household name in the West. As a matter of fact, Guangzhou officials are pondering ways to publicize the city through the Asian Games it will host soon. When the city gave up the old spelling, it threw its most valuable intangible property to the winds. Its biggest trading event is known overseas as the Canton Fair; Cantonese food is as widespread as McDonald's and KFC; people from Guangdong Province are called Cantonese. Now, if you ask most Americans about Cantonese, they are more likely to associate the name with Hong Kong.

Standardization is important. But the purpose is to make life easier, not to rigidly apply it to everything regardless of circumstances. As good as *pinyin* is, it is still a rule with exceptions. For example, we have Shanxi and Shaanxi, which – should *pinyin* be used – would be spelt the same unless we put tone marks above the letter *a*. Harbin did not give way to Ha'erbin.

Then, there are those cities in ethnic minority regions. Of course, you often see airlines fly to "Lasa" and "Wulumuqi", but the correct forms are Lhasa and Urumqi. For those who want every place name to appear as if they were typing it in a computer, my advice is: Learn it! Variety in culture is not a bad thing.

70. Those addresses, they keep changing

January 07, 2004

It used to be so simple.

Twenty-five years ago, before China opened its door to the caprices of the outside world, one could address anyone else by the ubiquitous *tongzhi* (comrade). Actually, it was de rigueur and carried a strong connotation of social equality.

If you addressed a sales lady as *xiaojie* (Miss), you might have got a stern look instead of a friendly smile and good service. At that time, *xiaojie* was tinged with old-time decadence and recalled the pre-1949 era of big-family melodrama.

mrade,
is is my lover.

Things have come full circle. If you speak Chinese, you are again advised not to use *xiaojie* indiscriminately. After gaining respectability as a courtesy title for women of noble birth or honorable pedigree, it has been gradually hijacked by the world's oldest profession as the default address for women who offer titillation or sex. "Miss, can I have a cup of tea" is more likely heard in a house of ill-repute than in a house of tasty food.

To counter the downward spiral of a once-lofty classification, people have come up with ingenious alternatives. Some retailers have begun to use *meinu* (beautiful woman) for any female customer. Preliminary reports reveal that it is producing small miracles as women who don't quite match up to the "beauty" tag feel so flattered that they end up buying more than they need.

The title as a compliment for good looks is bound to diminish in effectiveness if it turns into mainstream usage. Word choice is just like any other commercial product: the more people use it, the lower its social status. And when you push it to extremes, it may just boomerang back to hit you.

Take *laoban* (boss) for instance. It used to refer to owners of small or medium-sized businesses. It is still used in this sense, but patrons of all service industries, usually male, are increasingly addressed as such, even though they may not have a single share in any enterprise. Even government agencies have quietly joined the wordplay as officials, sometimes of very senior levels, are alluded to as *laoban* by their employees, usually behind their backs.

So, what happened to all the official titles, invariably ending with *zhang* and translated into "director" of various denominations?

They commanded deference, but in this day and age when the economy is overtaking politics as the focus of public attention, they have lost some of the bureaucratic grandeur. As market and law become dominant forces, fewer people will flaunt their official titles like championship trophies.

Meanwhile, businesses are more creative and customize for local or personal flavor in greeting clients. A chain restaurant serving northeastern cuisine has its waitresses welcome customers by calling them *dage* (big brother), which in China does not have any Orwellian undertones but conjures familial warmth. The same with *xiaomei* (little sister).

In Cantonese-speaking areas, *liangzai* (handsome boy) and *liangnu* (beautiful girl) can be used to address any young person. But would it sound sarcastic if one looks like the opposite of a prince charming or a cover girl?

Fortunately, irony and humor are seeping into this aspect of daily life. Some of the pejorative terms used in the Cultural Revolution, such as *heiwulei* (the black five categories), have taken on new meanings as preferred brand names.

Linguists must be having a field day chronicling all the changes and nuances of modern-day salutations. And purists are probably fuming over the subversion of dictionary-sanctified conventions. But those who use the language, native speakers or second-language users alike, may have something to discuss or digest when traffic jams become a boring topic.

As for *tongzhi* (comrade), the whiff of egalitarian utopia is giving way to a very definite and completely distinct denotation. It is now used within the gay community for mutual identification, and this applies in all parts of China, including Hong Kong and Taiwan.

71. A learning fad that's truly crazy

September 22, 2007

English as a second language (ESL) is all the rage in China. Gazillions of people are learning it. Unfortunately, the experience is quite unpleasant for many. Long hours and endless repetition of dry lessons yield little tangible result in terms of ability to use the language. No wonder the "I hate English" club is growing in leaps and bounds.

Into this chorus of grumbling stepped Li Yang, an entrepreneur who has invented his own pedagogy called "Crazy English". Simply put, he has his students stand in large formations and shout at the top of their lungs. It is designed to overcome the innate shyness of most Chinese in verbalizing what they have learned in the classroom or by themselves.

All this sounds innocent enough. But is it?

In recent weeks, Li Yang has incurred the wrath of the public after encouraging his students to kneel "in gratitude" towards him. Photos of a huge crowd in kowtow positions, first published by Li himself on his blog, raised the question: What's wrong with this person and his tactics?

The answer, in my opinion, is everything.

Li Yang is a demagogue, to say the least. He wants you to believe that he has come up with an effective way of learning a foreign language. But actually it is an excuse for mind control, intended to maximize his commercial interests. In addition to the exorbitant tuition fees, his overpriced books and tapes – many lifted from copyrighted materials – form the basis of his business empire.

Many students and their parents are deceived by him because they gain new confidence when they hear him preach. Like all demagogues, Li correctly identified a problem plaguing most ESL students in China.

The traditional method of learning words and grammar rules by rote has produced an army of students whose approach to the language is with a scalpel in hand. Many tend to use the language as if it were a dead one like Latin. One gets the feeling that it is a strange echo of the real language, sapped

of any vitality.

But saying the old way is wrong does not necessarily make the new way right. What the tongue-in-cheek "Crazy English" offers is truly crazy. The teaching sessions are like cult meetings; the shouting matches are reminiscent of the slogan fests during the Cultural Revolution. If shouting can improve one's linguistic skills, we would have all turned into Confucius after that mass movement.

Indeed, shouting breaks down psychological barriers and helps strengthen bonding. The question is: Is the new camaraderie used to inspire and learn, or to submit and be obedient? Can you question authority? Can you conduct a rational discourse?

Many reported a feeling of liberation at the "Crazy English" holler gatherings. That is not unique. The catch is, Li Yang liberates students in order to enslave them even further, very much like most agitators, political or commercial.

Even though our traditional methodology is fraught with rituals of submission, it has not stooped as low as asking hundreds of students to kneel as if they were being received by a feudal emperor. That is not a manifestation of a student's gratitude towards a teacher; rather, it strips a person of dignity and pounds him into obsequiousness.

Just imagine if Li had called his language education a "pyramid scheme" or "cult meeting" – what would have become of it? He is clever because he engages in these activities but adroitly avoids the label, of which many "regular" teachers of English have long accused him, at least in private.

After the kneeling incident, Li encouraged his female students to shave their heads. So far nobody has complied. But his true colors are now clear: he is crazy.

72. Make English learning less agonizing

July 01, 2006

A relative of mine was to graduate from college this summer. He was eyeing a job in international trade. But one day he asked me: "Why should a Chinese take time to learn a language that is not his own?"

No wonder he has difficulties. He is mentally against it in the first place.

"That is the stupidest comment I've ever heard," I thought of telling him. "It could have been propagated by those who want all the good jobs for themselves and would love to keep their competition at bay."

Of course, that would be using the same conspiracy theory that college kids are so often enamored with. Truth is, in this era of globalization, the ability to use English fluently significantly enhances one's job prospects. It is a skill just like any other.

It would be foolish to ask your suppliers, clients or people you come into contact with to learn Chinese because your competitors would gladly talk to them in their language. But on their part, the foreigners would certainly take the trouble to learn Chinese if the need warranted it. It is a business decision based on cost-benefit analysis, not one of national pride. The waves of Chinese learning English and outsiders learning Chinese attest to the ever-growing integration of China with the rest of the world.

Yet, it is undeniable that there are people in China who detest English-learning. Nationalism is

only an excuse. The real reason, as I suspect, is the way English is taught. The emphasis on memorization is such that no joy is left in the process, only endless irritation.

What students are presented in the classroom is not the language as it is used in real-life situations, but a dissection for anatomical study as if it were a corpse, grammatical niceties and all. The purpose is not to use the language in real-world communication, but to pass tests that prove you have this ability. Under normal circumstances, these two should mean the same. But it could be otherwise as shown in the following story.

A Chinese student with extremely high scores for American standardized tests was admitted into one of the Ivy League universities. But his professors soon found out that he could hardly understand them in the classroom. Suspecting that he cheated in the tests, school administrators demanded he repeat the tests. Again, he passed with flying colors. Not till then did they awaken to the reality that the student had mastered the techniques for acing the tests, not necessarily the skills demonstrated in them.

Come to think of it, there are special schools in China that promise to impart all the knowledge for attaining stratospheric scores in TOEFL, IELTS, GRE and others. The much-maligned annual Band 4 and Band 6 exams have become a hotbed for cheating because many test-takers do not work in areas where English is a necessary tool yet they have to do it for job promotion or for enrolment in certain programs.

Must English learning be such a pain in the neck?

On a recent trip to Copenhagen, I found most urban Danes spoke fluent English, with idiomatic word choices and little accent. Surprisingly, as I was told, they do not start their ABCs until the third grade, and in college only the English class is taught in English.

It is not a bilingual environment as I had thought. So, what has made them such good language learners? (Many of them speak German and other Scandinavian languages as well.)

"It is pop culture that has enabled us to pick up English in natural settings. We have many films, television shows and pop songs from English-language countries, and we don't dub them but only add Danish captions. That's the easiest way to learn," one explained to me.

China has a strong indigenous pop scene that demands most imports be dubbed, thus depriving us of the best resources of language teaching. But leaving a few channels of native-tongue programming would be feasible. Yet we would spend tens of billions of yuan and years of exertions on questionable pedagogy rather than simulating the most natural language platform short of moving to an English-speaking country.

And some of us would go so far as to devise a grand-sounding rationale for resistance.

Create an environment where learning English is natural and painless. Don't make it mandatory for people whose line of work does not require it. China will not become more international by adding millions of dabblers whose English proficiency amounts to a simple "Hello".

Chapter Eleven
When East and West interact

73. What is really behind a TV reality show?

July 07, 2007

It is always interesting to watch foreign media react to phenomena in China of such complexity that they do not fit into clear-cut Western interpretations. The television reality show is a case in point.

When *The Supergirls* first made it big in 2005, most domestic pundits saw a glimmer of democracy in the making as the wave of short-message votes swept candidates to instant popularity. On the other hand, several foreign commentators brushed aside the political implication and attributed the craze to behind-the-scenes maneuvering of business interests.

Now the tide has turned. A female director is described by The Times as daring to "defy both the will of the people and China's answer to Simon Cowell" when she said she might not cast the winners of a television contest show in a television drama series, as she was supposed to.

Let's pause for a moment and make an effort to define "the will of the people".

Do a million votes constitute "the will of the people"? What about five million? What if half the votes were cast by one person with deep pockets? What if the whole voting process was rigged by a producer who could make the Florida recount look like kid's play?

It seems outsiders are taking our television voting very seriously while we ourselves have long put it through the grinding machine of anything-for-entertainment. Try telling the story of *The Quiz Show* to a Chinese television viewer, and a likely response would be: "What's the big deal?"

I cannot tell you for sure which of China's reality shows is corrupt. Last year, someone successfully predicted the winner of one of the top rated shows week after week – days before each competition was held. Just imagine what the chances were for an educated guesser to hit that kind of bull's-eye.

To make you Jimmy Carter wannabes more agog, some suggest this could be the stroke of genius – not by a renegade or a rival station, but by the producers themselves. In China's entertainment industry, most scandals are created by the defamed stars or their managers because it is a more effective way to get exposure, and exposure entails a higher asking price for the next project.

I once grilled a friend of mine from the inner circle of another reality show, and he gave me a quizzical look: "I can tell you responsibly that the voting was not fixed." He put special emphasis on the word "responsibly" as if he were imitating some official facing the press.

Of course, this was not proof one way or the other. On the other hand, it does not take a UN election observer to know someone tampered with the outcome. Just follow one episode and you'd get a feeling of who is buying votes in bulk and who is getting a nudge from the producer.

The crux is not whether the process of a reality show is fair and transparent – are you out of your mind to expect a thing like that in a seriously frivolous environment like ours? The real point is, why do producers pretend to be fair and transparent in the first place?

The answer is simple: It makes them more money. The illusion of democracy tends to create euphoria among the target audience so that they will be more willing to punch their cellphones to see their favorite candidates survive another round of contest. In China, reality programming rakes in more profits from paid votes than from advertising.

You may see a television contest as the rough copy of a democratic system, but it is more like a clownishly rotten copy.

74. Messages behind Gates' dinner

April 22, 2006

I wonder if Bill Gates agonized over the dinner prepared at his residence for Chinese President Hu Jintao. Did the richest man in the world ever consider the option of "going Chinese" and playing host as a typical super-rich Chinese guy would?

By that I mean wining and dining with at least two dozen courses. Since Gates' wealth is many times that of the wealthiest Chinese, maybe he would multiple the number of courses by that rate and make it, say, a nice and nifty 100 or an auspicious 99.

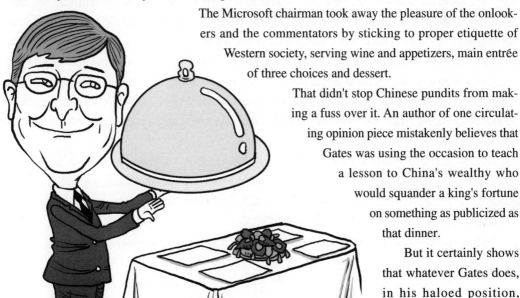

The Microsoft chairman took away the pleasure of the onlookers and the commentators by sticking to proper etiquette of Western society, serving wine and appetizers, main entrée of three choices and dessert.

That didn't stop Chinese pundits from making a fuss over it. An author of one circulating opinion piece mistakenly believes that Gates was using the occasion to teach a lesson to China's wealthy who would squander a king's fortune on something as publicized as that dinner.

But it certainly shows that whatever Gates does, in his haloed position, would be endlessly interpreted and imitated.

Thank God he didn't "customize" the dinner for the Chinese way of hospitality. It would have impressed all the Gates-wannabes in this country who will happily play catch-up and throw more lavish banquets than the ones they are already devouring, or more accurately, frittering away.

But Gates did intend to send one message through the meal, which he did by including Granny Smith apples and Walla Walla onions, which are local state produce. The feast was designed partly as a sampling of unique products from Seattle and the surrounding Pacific Northwest.

Too bad Microsoft Windows and Boeing 747 aircraft cannot be made into edibles. Or maybe they could. A Chinese chef could have carved miniature models of these made-in-Washington State products out of radish.

But I digress. To us Chinese, eating is not just about filling up the stomach. It is an art that we love to overindulge ourselves with. It may be the only art form that remains legal and yet savored by people across every social stratum.

The main reason we would overdo all these things is because we live in scarcity or constant fear of it. When one barely has enough to eat, he makes sure that once a year he can eat like there's no tomorrow.

There's a reverse correlation between abundance of food and conspicuous consumption of food. In the 1980s, whenever there was a buffet party, there would be people stuffing their pockets left and right. Fat chance you can find that today.

When I was in graduate school in China, a meal for a table of 10 at the campus restaurant would cost more than my monthly stipend. Yet I would never look at the table full of leftovers, let alone squirm over them. Then someone who returned from the United States asked for a plastic bag to take them home. We were aghast, and couldn't believe for a single second that it was a custom he had picked up from his overseas experience. We thought he had just found a lame excuse for being a miser.

You'll probably laugh it off as stupid if I say that banquets in China have grown less sumptuous in the past two decades. But in relation with the quantity and quality of food one consumes on a daily basis, it is definitely true. It is very rare today for a restaurant meal to set the epicure back an entire month's earning.

However, at many official functions, a feast still comprises a dozen or more courses. The first three are always the most delicious. Anything beyond the fifth course is increasingly transformed from gastronomic delight to palate and stomach workout. And not surprisingly, the higher the poverty level of the place, the higher the number of courses.

Maybe Gates should preinstall a Chinese version of his menu along with Windows.

75. Look into my eyes when you talk

December 22, 2007

What is the biggest cultural barrier for a Chinese to overcome when dealing with people from other countries?

For me personally, it is none other than looking into the eye of the other party. I knew early on while I was still in school that Western people value eye contact. But it is one thing to know something; it is another to be able to practice it.

It took me a good three years living in the United States to completely get over my "handicap". For a while, I invented a fence-sitting strategy whereby I would almost look at the person I was conversing with, but with a slight angle so that our eyes wouldn't be locked together at all times. I would appear to be looking without really looking.

Now you may ask: What's the big fuss about looking someone in the eye while talking to him? Isn't it the most natural thing to do?

Well, let me tell you: No, not for someone brought up and taught NOT to look that way. Actually, I've never encountered a specific instruction in our textbooks that we should not look directly at someone else while talking. And in school, we also look at the teacher. But when it's a one-on-one conversation, it is simply impolite to gaze, especially at someone of a senior generation or ranking.

This little habit of ours has probably created more misunderstanding than most cultural quirks. In Western culture, it is impolite to look at something other than the eyes of the one you talk to. Besides, you may be interpreted as lacking self-confidence or even lying.

Just imagine how many perfectly competent job candidates fell through this crack when recruiters from multinational companies took their Chinese way of politeness to mean the typical negative things associated with "not looking them in the eye".

Now, you may say that since we have rational knowledge of this behavioral discrepancy, why can't we adopt the Western way while talking to Westerners? Shouldn't that be easier than speaking a foreign language?

Easier said than done. Because "not looking" is so rooted in our cultural genes, during my transformative years, I constantly went through a process of internal struggle of "looking or not looking". I knew I should look, but just couldn't bring myself to it.

To understand how hard it is, you may have a little role-reversal and for once pretend you're a typical Chinese and look at the translator while talking to your host. If you feel comfortable, you can probably be a good actor.

Now let's take a step back. Suppose you cannot do that with ease just as you cannot take on a new accent at your will. You should pause for a moment when you see your Chinese friends engaging in the "wandering eye" and say to yourself: Hey, this guy may be a little shy, but he is not being discourteous because he grew up in a culture of discouraging such stares.

As for my personal experience, switching between looking and not looking is much harder than switching between two languages. After I came back to China as a "sea turtle", I could refrain from sprinkling my speech with English words, but I simply couldn't go back to looking sideways again.

Later, a friend scolded me for being "thoroughly Americanized" because my intent look was "too aggressive" and made him "nervous". I wish I could return to my "looking yet not looking" mode again, but no amount of theorizing can help me adjust with each occasion.

Habits die hard – good habits or bad. They make us who we are. Maybe we should all install a little mental translating device to remind ourselves of our little differences.

76. Applaud or not, that is the question

| August 25, 2007 |

If a tree falls in a forest and no one is around to hear it, does it make a sound?

Here is another dumb philosophical question: If you give a show and nobody applauds, is it a failure?

OK, I made the second one up. But it is a legitimate question.

If you've been to a few live performances in China, you'd think we have the worst performers in the world. If you've been to many, then you'd probably conclude we have the worst audiences.

You see, Chinese people who go to live entertainment rarely applaud, and the reason is much more complicated than you might imagine. First of all, we live in an age of cynicism. Whatever stunt you pull off, people are going to be blasé about it. I've seen Chinese acrobatic shows in both the US and China, and the audiences' reactions were as opposite as day and night. As a matter of fact, most acrobatic presentations in China nowadays are staged mainly for foreign tourists.

This mentality has made the job of impresarios, such as the producers of CCTV's Lunar New Year Eve gala and Zhang Yimou of "Olympic-Opening-Ceremony", more daunting than ever. How can you pique the interest of this been-there-seen-that crowd? This result is bigger, splashier production values and a cast of thousands.

In some places, a one-night-only act may cost more than 10 million yuan and is financed by the local government, which often pushes the cost down to local enterprises and even individuals. This is worse than regular white elephants like giant statues and plazas because the public doesn't even get to stroll around it every day.

A more latent culprit is the death of spontaneity. Many shows, especially those made for television, employ special "warm-up" guys who orchestrate the audience in totally contrived clapping and cheering of thunderous volume. The outpouring of exaggerated joy has served as an effective destroyer of the natural chemistry between performers and watchers. If you've been through a few of these well-

rehearsed applause fests, you'd probably feel it's a mechanical thing one does only when coerced.

That is not to say we Chinese people clap hands only ceremoniously. When you match the right show with the right audience, you'll get the variegated sounds that can be used to gauge the real reaction. But if you put a rock music lover into an opera house, you'd be lucky if he doesn't doze off.

You may ask: Why would a rock fan go to a classic opera in the first place? It's a long story. When China first opened up, entertainment was for everyone. People gobbled it up with no need of cultivating any discriminating taste. Just take a look at a television show from the early 1980s, and see the hearty laughs and cheers.

Then the market started to segment into niches. But it hasn't been backed up with sufficient information. There are people who attend a show mainly to flaunt their status or wealth. You'll see executive types in pop concerts fidgeting amid people one generation younger, or official types sitting through celebratory routines that they wouldn't go on their own even if you pay them a thousand bucks.

I once saw a grand function with an endless parade of celebrity entertainers. The applause was so sparse you'd think the audience had been drugged. Even the appearance of superstar Andy Lau triggered only a smattering of clapping. Now, if you fill the auditorium with 5,000 Yang Lijuan types, (remember the lady who drove her father to sell their house and then to suicide in order to finance her lunatic pursuit of Lau?) you'd bring the house down.

77. Spotlight on real China is not offensive

May 20, 2006

While a religious debate swirls around *The Da Vinci Code* as the movie premieres worldwide, another controversy surrounding another summer blockbuster has opened a can of worms in China, which may put in peril its fate in the market where the story is partly set.

Mission: Impossible III is under special scrutiny from the authorities because some media outlets have reported that it contains scenes that "tarnish the image of Shanghai".

That sounds weird. Hollywood filmmakers are bending backwards to enter the Chinese market, and who in his or her right mind would deliberately offend the audiences they are trying so hard to woo? It simply defies logic.

The Tom Cruise flick features three major locations, Shanghai being one of them. About 20 percent of the scenes were shot in the Chinese metropolis, using several landmark buildings as back-drops or sites of action sequences. The reportedly "offensive" scene catches traditional Shanghai homes hanging laundry outside the window.

What's so offensive about it, I wonder.

Doesn't Shanghai, or any other Chinese city, have such sights? Unless one isolates oneself in the kind of apartment buildings with an enclosed balcony, these are commonplace in traditional low-rises.

Does it reflect badly on a city?

I don't think one should be ashamed of hanging out cleaned-up laundry. Unless you live in a dry place like Beijing, you'd have to dry it in the open or buy a dryer, which is still rare in China. Sure, those who live in such quarters are not as well-off as residents of brand new and squeaky-clean apart-ment buildings, the practice is fundamentally different from spitting or jaywalking. It's something people do to keep hygienic, for God's sake.

This reminds me of the early 1980s when some of my countrymen were affronted when foreigners photographed Beijing's *hutong*. "It's sickening you would take interest in this kind of dilapidated

housing and choose to ignore the high-rises," they argued. It was difficult to convince them that the concrete boxes erected during that time were aesthetically unpleasing, and the *hutong*, rundown as they were from decades of neglect, had a quiet beauty that we, as insiders, were blind to.

The hypersensitivity toward how Chinese are portrayed in foreign films is rooted in a thinly veiled inferiority complex. Yes, there are movies that put us in a bad light, and yes, there are certain elements in foreign movies that may not suit our audiences. But if we hold every foreign production to the unique yardstick of a tourism publicity film, pretty soon people will avoid us and there will be no cinematic representation of our city on the international screen.

There is a possibility that some people think this is a good way of "driving away" foreign competition in Chinese cinema. If this is true, they are too naive. First of all, there is a quota for the annual number of foreign imports. If one film is cancelled, there will be a replacement. Second, when the film in question turns into a hot potato and needs "re-evaluation", its scheduled release date is changed. When that happens, the domestic distributor, who has invested millions in promoting it, may lose much of the value of paid publicity. The movie will also lose momentum and yield a significant portion of the market to bootleggers.

Worse yet, the movie, once approved again, may take another opening slot, which is usually planned in advance by some domestic release. That Chinese film, according to one of the biggest distributors in China, will lose all of its investment in marketing, since now it will unexpectedly face a Hollywood juggernaut.

About the only party who will benefit from this kind of hullabaloo are the movie pirates, who do not pay royalties to the filmmakers or taxes to the state coffers.

78. From Kundera to Dostoyevsky

December 01, 2007

You may have never known how much Fyodor Dostoyevsky and Milan Kundera had in common – until an Ang Lee movie changed one name for the other.

In *Eat, Drink, Man, Woman*, a story set in Taiwan, Lee's birthplace, local bookworms are nibbling at the novels of Kundera. But when the script reached James Schamus, Lee's New York-based writer-producer, Kundera morphed into Dostoyevsky.

It's not because the two novelists shared thematic or stylistic traits, but because the Russian writer occupies a place in the minds of American readers similar to that of the Czech-French in all parts of the Chinese reading public. An allusion to Kundera – or being caught reading his book, possibly in a fashionably decorated café – gives one a certain cachet, an implication that you are cool and belong to the hip crowd.

This is what I call a cross-cultural conversion.

A dictionary may help you translate words and names, but no tools – old-tech or hi-tech – can help you interpret the finer nuances of culture such as this one. All it takes is tons of knowledge and hands-on experience.

That is why Ang Lee's biography, recently published in the mainland after being reprinted 13 times in Taiwan, stands out so prominently. The book, which contains the above episode, brims with acute observations and sagely insight.

Even if you haven't seen any of Lee's movies – or if you don't like them – you'll find his words full of revelations. He is simply a marvel of cross-cultural jaywalking. He observes rules when he sees fit, but more often he creates new rules by opening up worlds we didn't even know existed.

A culture is like a universe all its own – a person can live in only one culture at any given time. But with the rapid pace of globalization, we need people who can hop between two universes and find parallels so that people from both sides can penetrate the glass partition of differences and communi-

cate in meaningful ways.

"Meaningful" communication suggests more than the surface meanings of words being uttered. I remember a speech President Clinton gave during one of his trips to China. It sounded great in English, but once rendered verbatim into Chinese, it was basically a jumble of gibberish.

A translator for diplomatic occasions does not have the leeway to change Kundera into Dostoyevsky. And I'm not implying formal speeches given by Chinese leaders are easily accessible to a Western ear either.

When we speak or act, we invariably take a position that conforms to our own culture. It takes an expert like Ang Lee, who straddles both cultures and knows the strengths of each, to communicate in a meaningful way. When you read the English subtitles of *Crouching Tiger, Hidden Dragon*, for example, you're actually not reading a word-for-word translation of the original Chinese, but what the characters might say if their native language were English.

Now, I must add that we don't even have enough good translators to convert Kundera into Kundera, let alone to Dostoyevsky. Our "proctology hospital" shows up as "anus hospital", and "spring chicken", a popular item in Chinese restaurants overseas, is decoded into "chicken without sexual life".

But we need people who are able to decipher the nuances of culture, who can translate the cultural significance of Kundera into Dostoyevsky. Hunan Satellite Television has grasped that skill – it makes huge hits by localizing foreign reality programming. The Chinese hosts of David Beckham, on the other hand, have not. They treated him to a lavish banquet full of outlandish dishes like fried scorpions. The football star didn't even touch it.

79. When aesthetic standards diverge

January 19, 2008

The coming Oscars ceremony may be threatened by the ongoing writers' strike, but Chinese entertainment reporters and cineastes have one less reason to worry about it. This week, it was announced that all three Chinese language movies submitted for Best Foreign Language Picture consideration – from the Chinese mainland, Hong Kong and Taiwan – failed to get on the nine-nominee shortlist.

This may not say much about the quality of these films. Voting for a best artistic work is capricious at best because art, as beauty, is often in the eye of the beholder. Case in point: this year, many of the most promising movies – the Chinese submissions not included – were snubbed in this category.

We may not like to admit it, but we look towards Western confirmation for the excellence of Chinese films, or the lack of it. Chen Kaige did not become a "master" until his *Farewell, My Concubine* took the coveted Palme d'Or. Zhang Yimou did not secure his status until he was consistently lauded by the big three European awards.

Our lack of an aesthetic authority or standard of our own is the result of many factors: Our own

prizes are often pretenders. They may be preceded by lavish stage productions, but the selection process is opaque and whatever yardsticks that can be detected smack of outdated mentalities. Our entertainment press rarely looks beyond the box-office champions, and our academic journals are laden with second-hand research at least 20 years out of sync with the times.

Most of all, we do not have the self-confidence to assert our own aesthetic standards when it comes to our own artistic work.

We Chinese have a saying: "A flower blossoms outside the wall, and its fragrance wafts into the courtyard." That means, you'll have to leverage outside forces to build your name inside. That is good when a genius is overlooked at home and trumpeted overseas. If you reverse the equation, things no longer look good.

Cultural differences exist, even in this age of globalization. In the 1980s, a widely acclaimed Chinese movie, *My Memory of Old Beijing*, aspired for an Oscar and failed to make the grade. Nobody in China lamented. The film had such a quintessential Chinese style that it was only natural that outsiders did not pick up the nuances. If we left the selection of the greatest Chinese fiction to Western experts, *Dream of the Red Mansions* would never make the cut.

I'm not advertising a psychological balancing act by discounting the significance of Western accolades, an attitude many Chinese filmmakers have adopted in their frustration over their perceived neglect. What I'm saying is, we should know what is good Chinese art even when outsiders do not recognize it because we live in this country and live the aesthetic values espoused by these works.

One way to assert our cultural identity is to introduce to the outside world what is truly good and great in our literary and artistic canon, not what suits the current political winds. Familiarize opinion leaders such as media critics, academics, agents and impresarios with these works. Their attention has been drawn to those we tend to demonize. Beijing's 798 art community was almost demolished until it became a favorite destination for foreign visitors. And honestly, many of our official submissions to the Oscars are so mediocre that I wonder if those in charge of the selection process have any clue of what is universally considered high quality.

Do not get carried away when our traditional arts get respect. It is more important that they are understood and appreciated. Italian opera is performed all over the world – often by non-Italians; in comparison, Peking Opera is like museum art.

80. Skin-deep translation may mislead

May 09, 2008

To translate a word from one language to another is easy; to translate a context is hard.

The New York Times carried an article in its May 4 book review that called Guo Jingming "the most successful writer in China". That must have pleased millions of Guo's fans, but it surely shocked a lot more people.

"How can NYT stoop so low?" many asked.

Guo is currently the bestselling author in China and, by correlation, the highest earning one as well. But the 24-year-old is not respected. He was found by a court of law to have committed the cardinal sin for a writer – plagiarism. But, against the court order, he refused to apologize, explaining that he needed to uphold his image in the eyes of his adoring fans.

Apart from this, nobody is praising his adolescent schmaltz for literary achievement.

All this was sketched out in detail in the NYT essay. But whoever first reported it in the Chinese press did not bother to read the whole article. He or she was so focused on the word "successful" that everything else probably became a blur.

From the NYT article, it is natural to deduce that the author meant "commercial success". However, the Chinese translator-cum-commentator has obviously interpreted it as "literary excellence" or "high quality overall".

In an ideal world, a work of great literary value should have high sales. But we don't live in an ideal world, and bestsellers, like blockbuster movies, do not necessarily do anything except fill a few hours of your leisure time.

The misunderstanding of NYT's appraisal of China's literary pop idol is more evident when the context is enlarged from the article to the whole book review section. On that day, NYT carried four full-length reviews of four Chinese novels: *Wolf Totem* by Jiang Rong, *Life and Death Are Wearing Me Out* by Mo Yan, *The Song of Everlasting Sorrow* by Wang Anyi and *Serve the People* by Yan Lianke – all serious works by accomplished writers. The Guo Jingming piece was like a dessert, nice and frothy, but not able to replace the main entrees.

None of the Chinese commentators mentioned any of the four book reviews. Through endless copying and reposting, which is the pillar of Chinese website management, the point has been hammered home that Americans, for whatever unfathomable reason, favor China's most ridiculed literary pretender as their favorite Chinese writer.

There are commentators who suspect the NYT piece was being sarcastic in its choice of words, countering "most successful" with a detailed description of Guo's less-than-flattering acts, but you won't be able to go into that much depth from the headlines or the opening paragraphs. As we know, website editors have a flair for creating outrageous headlines that hardly correspond to the general idea of the article.

This is a perfect example – albeit innocuous – of what I call "cultural mismatch". It's more than getting lost in translation. It's about picking up only what interests you and leaving behind everything else, including the right perspective and right context. It can happen between two languages and two cultures, but also between two demographic groups.

An American writer once noticed that street kids were wearing a special badge as part of a necklace. He thought it was a sign for peace and was heartened. It turned out they were insignia from brand-name automobiles, the preferred object of theft among that group.

Another ridiculous misinterpretation was made by a reporter from a big-name American magazine. He paid us a visit during his trip to China. Later, he wrote that the security guards at our building were here to intimidate us into self-censorship. At such skin-deep observation, I couldn't help but laugh.

Chapter Twelve
When East and West Collide

81. A Chinese has no right to sculpt Martin Luther King?

September 08, 2007

Lei Yixin is not a household name in China. Even when he was selected as the sculptor for a monument to Martin Luther King Jr. to be erected at the National Mall in Washington DC, it did not make the front pages of the Chinese press.

But in the United States, the news has sparked controversy. To put it mildly, a group of African American artists are questioning the wisdom of choosing an Asian – even a non-American – for such

a high-profile project. And to back up their argument, they have mixed politics with personal sentiments.

I can understand why they are not happy with the selection, which, by the way, was done by a 12-member committee, 10 of whom were African American. When three Chinese actresses were selected for major roles in the Hollywood movie *Memoirs of a Geisha*, some Japanese actresses were just as upset. By the same token, when a French architect was chosen to design China's National Theater, you can imagine how many of his Chinese counterparts were displeased.

It is difficult to tell whether the reason is one of nationality.

The defense for picking someone ethnically unaligned with the subject of portrayal is usually on technical grounds: the Chinese actors could speak better English, or Lei the sculptor has a better grasp of realism.

I am sure there are myriad reasons for someone like Lei to have been selected over African American artists who competed and who no doubt were competent. Technical skill is just one consideration.

I am no expert on fine arts, but to illustrate my point, here is an example.

When Grace Bumbry was cast in a Wagner opera in Bayreuth in 1961, people were stunned. Wieland Wagner, grandson of the composer, said it was "the color of her vocal tone, not the color of her skin that counts". After that, opera gradually became color-blind, to the extent that a singer of African descent could play the role of Desdemona on the same stage with a Caucasian singer – in blackface – in *Othello*.

I do not believe Wieland Wagner was oblivious to Bumbry's skin color. In the early years when singers of African descent were cast in non-black roles, it was more of a statement that people of color should not be barred from this pantheon of European high culture. That they were artistically brilliant was of secondary importance.

You may say theater is make-believe. In 1989 Jessye Norman, another great African American singer, was invited to sing La Marseillaise, the French national anthem, in Paris during the celebration of the bicentennial of the French Revolution. This would be tantamount to the Beijing Olympics having a foreign vocalist to sing the theme song.

One possibility that can be ruled out is that the home country did not have the right talent for the occasion. My assumption is, the French wanted to imply that even though it was a quintessentially French celebration, it was also something to be shared with the whole world.

We live in a global village, yet we also need to preserve our national and ethnic identity. It could become a balancing act. What does an artist stand for? His ethnicity? Nationality? Artistic merit? Political belief? A different perspective?

To come back to the King statue, it would be equally valid to assign the work to an African American artist or a non-black, non-American one. An African American sculptor may understand King better, but an outsider may provide a fresh look.

And just imagine what extra good it could do if this project gets more Chinese to know about Martin Luther King and what he stood for. Someone like King who preached universal love and understanding should be for everyone.

82. Men from China in a bull shop

November 24, 2007

Chinese tourists being photographed riding Wall Street's famous Charging Bull has sparked a controversy in China. A Beijing Television reporter spotted the scene and lamented in her blog about the lack of civilized behavior among some of our countrymen.

Once again, netizens played sleuths, but this time for evidence against the reporter. They reposted photos of Western tourists on top of the same bull, adding that this particular piece of sculpture is open for "riding".

Wikipedia notes that the Wall Street Bull was actually not commissioned by the New York government, but a result of "guerilla art". It was created and installed by someone named Arturo Di Modica, who still owns it. The entry does not mention whether it is okay for an ordinary tourist, obviously without the prior approval of either the sculptor or the city, on whose land it sits, to ride it.

Therefore, I cannot come to a conclusion whether a tourist, Chinese or otherwise, is behaving inappropriately if he or she does it. But I'm not surprised the reporter thought that way. It is often reported that some Chinese tourists have bad manners while traveling overseas.

I've witnessed it several times. I don't think they're deliberately "destroying the image of China". Instead, I deem it a continuation of long-wrought bad habits. If you go to a popular tourist attraction in China and wait for your turn for an ideal photo spot, you may never get it. You'd have to bull your way into it.

I don't think a single Chinese can represent the whole country. There are many who take efforts to observe local customs. But, if too many carry on their indecorum wherever they go, it's bound to happen that some outsiders may view us – all of us – in a negative light.

That's why we need education campaigns to change those behaviors. And we should start from home. Let's refrain from the traditional thinking that a personal faux pas would mar the national image. Let's create the notion that a good citizen should not act improperly, whether in Waihuan Street or Wall Street. Netizens are wrong to infer that it is appropriate to do something simply because others, possibly locals, are doing it. Would you rob someone if you see a robber doing it without getting caught?

That said, some sculptures on public land are indeed for "interaction". I was walking in a park in Yixing, Jiangsu Province, the other day and spotted a couple of boys frolicking on top of a sculpture. As soon as I pointed my camera at them, they turned stiff and an old gentleman who wore a park badge started shouting at them. I asked him whether he would leave them alone if I, a reporter, had not shown an interest in them. He nodded. What the kids were doing was "naughty" to him, but a symbol of innocence to me.

To take the bull of manners by the horns, I offer the following advice: If you want to ride that famous bull to ensure you'll be part of a future bull run, look for signs first. If they have words like "No climbing", don't do it. Take photos in front of it instead. Since most sculptures on public land do not allow body contact, so to speak, you can assume the default rule is "No". If you find words to the contrary, from either posted notices or nearby security guards, go ahead, why not have fun with it?

Better use delicacy while tackling a bull than be a bull in a china shop.

83. Zhao Yan beating case

September 24, 2005

A Chinese tourist looking around the Niagara Falls near the US-Canadian border was severely beaten by a US security officer.

That was basically what happened on July 21, 2004, and it was how facts are presented and shape public opinion, including influencing jurors that deserve attention.

When the bruised face of Zhao Yan appeared in the media a year ago, it sent a shockwave among the Chinese public – and rightly so. What did she do to have deserved such cruel treatment? However, in the subsequent rainstorm of denunciations posted on popular websites, there was rarely any judicious analysis. Many simply jumped to the conclusion that the officer did it out of malice for Chinese people per se, not thinking that there are many other nationals who look like Chinese in the American eye, let alone the tens of millions of Asian-Americans.

There seemed to be a distinct line between traditional media and the new media in reflecting this unfortunate incident. While the "old school" tended to adhere to journalistic principles and reported on

how the Chinese and the US governments dealt with the matter, some "new kids on the block" took the sensational route, eliciting wholesale condemnation and stereotyping.

Police brutality could certainly be a justifiable issue here, but cultural differences may have played a bigger role. To Zhao Yan, the 38-year-old businesswoman from Tianjin, it seemed an intuitive response to flee from someone who was chasing her. It may not even matter how she would have reacted in a similar situation in China because all the Hollywood movies could have conditioned her to take off.

To Robert Rhodes, the US Homeland Security officer charged with violating Zhao's civil rights and recently acquitted in the criminal case, it was his duty to arrest someone who fit the description of a drug-trafficking suspect and, when Zhao fled and reached for something in her bag, used all means to stop her. There have been frequent reports in the US of hesitant or lenient cops who ended up being killed in the line of duty by those they were trying to detain.

Did Rhodes use excessive force? It appeared so from the photo. But again, we must examine the circumstances of how one thing led to another. Each one gave an account that was favorable to his or her own argument, which did not really surprise anyone. Assuming each was telling the truth, it may not be the whole truth. Rhodes' track record may shed light on whether he has a penchant for "excessive force".

We must admit that the jurors had a ringside seat on the facts. I respect their verdict, but that did not reduce my sympathy for Zhao. She may not have acted wisely, but how could she know better? It is ludicrous to expect her to act like an American the minute she descended on the land. That's why the word "tourist" has certain connotations.

Public perception towards Zhao Yan took a sharp turn when someone leaked that hers was a government-paid pleasure trip disguised as a business trip. Online responses were swift and vicious: "She deserved the beating and it served her right," many wrote.

One could not help but marvel at the hatred that Chinese people have for corruption. However, who footed her travel bill and who was her employer is totally irrelevant to this case. The same goes for the defendant's claim that she had violated her visa restrictions by engaging in activities not allowed by her visa type. Even if she had jumped ship and was in the US illegally, she should not be treated inhumanely. That is the bottom line.

My deduction is, those who were exhilarated to see a "damned corrupt person" beaten were the same ones who had earlier felt the whole Chinese nation was insulted. When news was presented in a sensational form, it certainly evokes simplistic responses. While it is good to care about one's compatriots, especially when they are away from the homeland, it may not be rational to equate an isolated incident with a full-blown bilateral confrontation.

Sensationalizing the Rodney King beating did not help America's racial relations. Nor will this case for justice or Sino-US relations.

84. Kenneth Eng's racist lunacy

│ *March 17, 2007* │

There is a furor in the Asian-American community. It was caused by an article entitled "Why I Hate Black People" by Kenneth Eng, which was published last month in the San Francisco-based newspaper AsianWeek.

Now, I won't quote from it or link to its Web page, which was removed by the paper anyway. But the content in graphic or text form is floating in cyberspace, sparking heated debate and denunciation. And two more of Eng's opinion pieces are still available: "Proof That Whites Inherently Hate Us" and "Why I Hate Asians".

Eng is a self-proclaimed "Asian supremacist", proud of his racial bigotry and despising those Asians who do not conform to his standards of the Asiam "master race". If you ponder his logic, he hates everyone except those as deluded as he is. That's why no sensible Asian could possibly side with him even though he puts Asians on the top of his racist stack.

If one agrees with his logic that one race is innately superior, it will soon follow that one place, one gender, one type of physique is destined to be the greatest – the "one", the "savior" of the human race, so to speak. Doesn't that sound familiar?

It would be so easy to laugh him off as a joke. But the case of Kenneth Eng offers us a chance to look into the soil, both social and psychological, that breeds this second coming of nation-destroying racist lunatics of every skin color.

In the US, Asians have traditionally kept a low profile. As late as half a century ago, they could not have interracial marriages; and even now they have a hard time breaking into pop culture. It wouldn't be a far stretch to presume that Eng suffers from a persecution complex and tries to overcompensate it with an armor of pre-emptive attacks.

His stereotyping of black Americans is so ugly that you won't see anything like it in a public arena of discussion. But Eng is obviously not alone. Echoes of his sophomoric intolerance can be found anywhere, including here in China. Some international schools reject blacks whose native language is English, and hire whites whose first language is not, as English language tutors. This is dictated by the pupils' parents, according to the reports.

Most people harbor some form of racism. Yet, most people are good-hearted and will counter it with common sense and growing understanding. In Guangzhou, when Africans arrived to conduct business a couple of years ago, they were sometimes avoided like the plague on buses. But with more of them coming to town, it is rare nowadays for locals to view them with suspicion.

It is not cause for alarm that a ranting and lurid racialist like Eng has burst on the scene. Any society, no matter how harmonious, always has freaks on its fringes. It should be a concern when such blatant hatred goosesteps into the mainstream.

When I browse Internet forums and blogs here, I'm under the constant impression that we have millions of Kenneth Engs spewing fire and poison like an army of deranged dragons. They start by hating people from Henan Province because some egregious crimes happened there. Then they denounce any place that receives negative news coverage or any people whose opinions differ from theirs.

It is saddening if this is a glimpse of free expression. I'm sure it cannot represent the majority of the Chinese people, but when you get vociferous enough you can drown out the rational voice. Well, at least in San Francisco, AsianWeek promptly dismissed Eng and issued an apology.

I believe that Eng's rant, dangerous as it is, should not be muzzled. We need to be aware what type of world we live in. The question is, how can we keep the uninitiated from being infected by such demagoguery?

85. Virginia Tech killing

April 19, 2007

The shooting rampage at Virginia Tech on Monday shocked the world. My thoughts and prayers are with the families and the community that suffered this senseless tragedy. Anyone with even a modicum of human compassion would feel the same.

It is only natural for people to be curious about the identity of the gunman. However, in the quest for truth, there is a disturbing sign of linking an individual act with something larger.

As long as the killer did not represent any group or harbor any political motive – as seems to be the case – any suggestion about his ethnicity will only add insult to injury and death. The rumor that he was Chinese before police positively identified him is indicative of a troubling trend, both in the US and in China, that one person, good or bad, somehow personifies a whole community, even a whole nation.

Some US media commentators' implications

based on his ethnicity were not only unprofessional but insidious. If he were Chinese, did that mean Chinese people are intrinsically hostile to the US? Or that an average Chinese would act that way?

In a strange way, this reaction is reciprocated here in China. When news came that the killer was not Chinese, people heaved a collective sigh of relief. If you analyze the underlying logic, it means that his being Chinese would have incriminated all of us. Now that he was not, a few would say: "We Chinese would never do a crazy thing like that."

The truth is, a lone killer with no agenda could be of any ethnicity. We have our share of these loners, including Lu Gang, who gunned down several of his schoolmates and teachers on a US campus, and Ma Jiajue, who hacked several of his classmates with a machete.

Any society, no matter how well-balanced and harmonious, cannot be totally devoid of these people. They can never represent the society that they live in or that brought them up. Equating them with the society at large is to impugn innocent people who happen to share the killers' traits such as ethnicity or profession. It is guilt by association – association of the most untenable kind.

I can understand why some would resort to such simplistic reasoning. The tragedy is so enormous that it is sometimes hard to reckon with the cause without further embellishing it. How can one crazy person mow down so many others, people he probably didn't even know?

While there is no way we can totally rid the world of such elements, there are, I believe, ways to minimize their damage.

One is psychological aid, especially for those who, shut in a cocoon of their own, have difficulty communicating with others and have no outlet for releasing negative energy. In the US, postmen are said to be more vulnerable than other professions. In China, college students should receive more counseling. Sometimes, it is up to peers to reach out to those who do not seek help.

Then, there is the easy availability of guns in America. While I fully respect US citizens' constitutional right to own guns, we must recognize that, in cases like the Virginia Tech incident, the use of guns was a crucial factor. If the killer did not have guns, he would probably have killed only a few people and could have more easily been constrained by others. It is not an exaggeration that it became the deadliest killing spree on an American campus mostly because he had two handguns, legally purchased.

We will never live in a world where everyone is happy and treats others with respect. That's a utopian ideal. But we can at least limit gun access so that one person won't be able to inflict destruction on a massive scale.

86. Exporters between rock and hard place

September 29, 2007

It is risky to defend an unpopular cause, such as the recent product scares involving Chinese exporters. There is an old saying that epitomizes the ideal response: "If you made the mistake, go correct it. If not, take it as a warning."

Things are more complicated in reality. Every case is unique. You don't know where the buck should stop. But that is something against the nature of journalists ready to spot a trend out of a few isolated incidents.

If you delve deeper, a product defect could come from one of several origins: it could be a lapse in design, a blunder in manufacturing, or even incompatible standards. Within the realm of manufacturing, a failing could be an honest mistake, a slip-up, a systematic attempt to cut corners, or a lack of quality control so pervasive that nothing can be guaranteed.

It is not surprising that, of the large amount of products shipped from China, a small percentage is tainted with quality deficiencies. Quality control programs such as the six-sigma are designed to reduce the rate of defects. No manufacturer can guarantee that everything he produces can be totally safe from flaws.

I've used half a dozen notebook computers since the product category came into being, and they were all big-name brands. Without exception, they all failed at one time or another. If I draw a conclusion from my experience, I should probably never buy another notebook.

Sound ridiculous? That is the same as campaign of "China-free" labeling, meaning the product has no parts whatsoever made in China, and therefore with no quality problems.

Granted, China has a long way to go to improve its quality management. But we should be fair that it has also come a long way in the past 30 years. Like the economy itself, the product quality of a developing country usually starts at a low level and moves up the ladder. That was true of both Japan and South Korea.

All this sounds like a lame excuse to defend one's own country, right?

Actually, I'm very much in favor of consumers, both domestic and foreign, constantly pounding manufacturers for quality improvement. The bottom line: no product should be allowed into the market that may bring harm to the consumer.

That said, I must add a word for Chinese manufacturers who sell abroad. I've talked to many who said they are caught between a rock and a hard place: They want to raise quality standards, but at the same time they are under extreme pressures to lower costs.

The pressure comes from Western buyers and their agents, who cut prices so low that profits diminish and evaporate. Now China has also been accused of dumping. But nobody wants to sell low. Nobody wants to work all year round and earn nothing, or even lose money.

You'll say, "It's a free market, and nobody is forcing you to sell at that price." That's right, but as the laws of economics indicate, when buyers are big and powerful while sellers are small and replaceable, the latter are not really in a position to bargain. You are lucky if you get an order and keep the factory humming and the workers fed. Sometimes you'll have to take a shipment as free or heavily discounted samples that would hopefully bring profitable business later.

Businesses exist to make money. When buyers overpower sellers into accepting a price that eliminates a reasonable profit margin, they are essentially accomplices in a scheme to play fast and loose in quality.

There are big businesses that prefer an ethical facade and assign the dirty job to trading companies. However you play it, if you cut prices as if cutting throat, you should expect others to cut corners in quality.

87. Gun-toting French executive

September 01, 2007

When an expatriate manager goes bananas over a small incident, does it signify something larger?

The Southern Metropolis Daily, a Guangzhou-based newspaper, reported that the French manager of a Dongguan company pulled out a pistol and fired a shot at the ceiling during a meeting. "Pierre", who manages a French-invested manufacturer of wood products, carries a gun and is not afraid to use it. According to several workers' accounts, he had fired shots on at least three occasions, mostly to draw attention or calm down an unruly crowd.

The paper could not reach Pierre for confirmation. But it did talk to the local police, who said they had to report to higher authorities before determining how to pursue the case because it involved a foreign citizen.

As you can imagine, this has unleashed another spate of anti-foreign-employer sentiments. One media comment was simply titled, "How can foreigners run wild in China?"

While this is certainly not the first reported case of abuse by a foreign manager or employer, it is by far the strangest. Previously it was a Korean or Japanese manager who resorted to harsh disciplinary measures in dealing with Chinese employees, but this Pierre acted as if he were a little Napoleon wielding absolute power in his own mini-kingdom.

Let me add that I'm assuming everything in the report is true, since I cannot verify it independently. This is a small technicality that many readers tend to ignore. Some of my earlier columns aroused controversies because readers skipped over my claim of assumption.

If the report is to be believed, what Pierre did was insane, not to mention illegal. In China, only very select authorized groups are allowed to carry firearms. This trigger-happy French executive reminds one of some notorious despots who made overdramatic scenes with their power. Coincidentally, Pierre did not leave until one of the "smart" guys at the meeting started applauding him while the rest sat "stunned". This could be a scene from a movie.

Could something like this happen in the real world, in the 21st century? If it did happen, as the paper said it did on August 18, the reason is other than the kind of "foreign superiority" that netizens and online pundits denounce, but kowtowing to whoever controls one's fate. The nationality of a person with this kind of braggadocio is of little relevance, if any. It is essentially an employer-employee relationship that is at the core of this incident and is warped beyond belief.

The Chinese people can put up with a lot of abuse. Some people call it "resilience" and deem it a virtue. Some private enterprises employ quasi-military management styles. We've all seen restaurant workers being lined up and "trained" as if they were soldiers. And we've heard of some lines of workers, such as waiters and hair-washers, being ordered to render their services while kneeling down.

Even in the US, Chinese-run businesses have been reported to defer payment and otherwise act in violation of labor laws and ethics. Even today, there is still the lingering notion that a non-State-owned enterprise could be Dickensian in treating its employees.

Fortunately, in the past decade, we have gained a heightened sense of employee rights. More and more people have the guts to stand up to abusive bosses, whether Chinese or expatriate. While the legal environment is working in their favor, another factor is against them. If your job is highly replaceable, you'll be amazed how much maltreatment you can take. And it's not just a Chinese characteristic.

When employees are armed with legal knowledge, a gun-toting boss will think twice before going berserk.

Chapter Thirteen
In the Mood for Humor

88. A sure-fire plan to lure pirates to my books

August 03, 2007

A funny thing happened to me yesterday. A friend of mine MSNed me, mentioning that a book I wrote two years ago was available for download on a certain website.

It took me by surprise. I had licensed the digital version of two earlier reference books to a database, which should not appear in book format. I clicked to the offending site and found several of my essay collections hyped for free downloading.

My friend, intrepid investigative reporter that he is, waded through the convoluted process and spotted a scam. But to do that, he had to present his cellphone number, and minutes later, a small chunk of kuai disappeared from his account. He made a lot of calls and inquiries, and in the end, he failed to access anything except a brief introduction to my volumes. The unscrupulous operator was just using my books as a bait, he concluded. I was at once relieved and dismayed. How can I be upgraded to the status of a plagiarism-worthy author? For me, it

would be like winning the Nobel Prize – almost, but with more street cachet.

"They should have stuck with Han Han. He could get them more suckers in a day than I can in a year," I grumbled, suggesting the photogenic, establishment-busting best-selling author-cum-race car driver.

I've published a dozen books, but they sold like cold cakes on a freezing day. I've always wondered how to increase sales short of threatening to jump off a skyscraper and creating media awareness.

Actually, I know how to write a profitable book. I can put out pamphlets to impart my boundless knowledge of learning English, including how to get a full score of TOEFL by cheating, of which I had been accused – groundlessly, I should add. Those titles take one week to finish and can sell to an endless stream of new buyers as each generation is given the fresh headache of linguistic globalization in an artificially agonizing pedagogy.

I can accept translation work. I tend to reject all such gigs. That has upset the few who admire my bilingual writing. I have my reason: I can't help embellishing with such abandon that it amounts to rewriting. After I put my usual touch of genius on a piece of literature, the original author was so flattered that he would consider offering me the byline.

Or I can write scripts for movies and television drama. For that, I need to dumb myself down and get into a kitschy mode, which I picked up in San Francisco. Instead of writing "I'm happy", I'll dramatize it to "I'm so happy I'm fainting and I cannot get up." Chicks fall for this stuff. All I need is to wax sentimental every five minutes and dictate that actors emote profusely.

Or I can go for the adolescent market and churn out sexual fantasies. China's testosterone-surging netizens will turn me into an instant star. All I need is the Letter page of Playboy and I'll never run out of details. Yes, I should give up column writing and get into creative writing. I bet my books will be pirated hot off the press.

89. Year of the Pig

August 26, 2007

This is the Year of the Pig. We Chinese are supposed to turn the animal into a lovey-dovey pet. But, no! In spite of all the colorful piggy banks that are sold in souvenir stores, we still have a love-hate relationship with the pig.

When used figuratively, "pig" is predominantly pejorative. In English, someone who is called "a pig" is greedy or gross. The Chinese connotation is slightly different. A pig evokes three images: gluttonous, lazy and dirty. The "lazy" part is a contrast with the Western interpretation. If you're slothful, you cannot be too avaricious, right?

You thought only you could fly?

Cool!

Well, obviously, it is a nicety that does not bother linguists. The bottom line is, don't call anyone a pig, in either English or Chinese or banter, because it'll be an insult.

But wait! A friend of mine calls himself "flypig". An entertainment reporter from South China uses "milk pig" as her handle. If you browse the Internet, you'll come across many who gladly take on the pot-bellied swine as their identification. And these people belong to the cool generation.

Yet, the same netizens rose up in angry protests when a scholar released a study titled "Chinese are the descendents of the pig". Huang Shouyu uncovered a slew of totem images and concluded that primeval Chinese worshipped the porcus omnivorous. (I'm trying to be pompous here.)

The reason? It was seen as intelligent, aggressive and virile. That was before they were domesticated and bred for human consumption, of course. The virility part actually seeped into the Chinese zodiac. Just witness the boomlet of piglets this year and imagine all the overcrowded classrooms a decade from now, and you'll understand why people love to pop into this world when all the pigs are lined up.

Contrary to the scholar's interpretation, children born in the Year of the Boar are believed to be easy going, sincere, tolerant, honest and naive. Does that sound implausible? Well, these traits could be a positive spin of lazy, fat and filthy.

But I digress. Professor Huang antagonized the online public because they grew up with "We're descendents of the dragon" honed into the psyche. Huang contends that it dates back only 30 years, when two pop jingles from Hong Kong and Taiwan popularized the myth of the dragon.

Honestly, I did not read through his thesis, which is long and filled with archaic terms and citations. I just feel that the dragon is so cool and, even though it has slayers chasing on its tail, it will never be someone's bacon, which, I guess, is a bigger fear than being accused of bad smell. On top of it, dragons fly regularly, and probably don't require a passport and a visa, whereas pigs fly, well, when pigs fly.

I wonder if the pig will ever rise in stature to rival the dragon. Perhaps when some of the pig-named young are crowned with celebrity halo, they'll call themselves "Li Little Pig" or "Becoming Pig" to offset the legacy of Bruce Lee and Jackie Chan.

In the meanwhile, the pig will be a polarizing figure, somewhat like Hillary Clinton, who by chance was born in a Year of the Pig.

90. The Louisiana Purchase

March 15, 2007

Spending Lunar New Year outside China is no fun. No firecrackers. No strings of red lanterns. No endless feasts to grow fat enough for a year of hibernation.

But my family lives only hours from New Orleans, the city whose "dragon temple was destroyed by a flood" a year and half ago, to borrow the literal meaning of a Chinese idiom. This year, its Mardi Gras overlapped in time with the Chinese festival. So, I decided to take my family to get a Creole coating of our New Year's celebration.

Mardi Gras is all about beads, or necklaces with faux pearls more colorful and sparkling than the real thing. In antediluvian times, a spectator had to do something outrageous to get free beads. Usually, women would tantalize by revealing part of their top so that those wearing masks on the floats would reward them with baubles.

But to boost sagging tourism, thousands of glitter-

The Earth is spinning backwards! Go buy properties!

ing trinkets are thrown into the crowd and that's just for one float on one parade route.

It was my first trip to Louisiana, and I took time gazing at the Mississippi River levees and posing in front of oak-lined old mansions. Wow, everything within my sight was acquired from Napoleon Bonaparte by the United States for $15 million. That sum can barely get you a condo at Tomson Riviera on the Huangpu River in Shanghai, the self-acclaimed most expensive residential property in China.

That is, if you don't take inflation over the years into account.

Actually the Louisiana Purchase in 1803 included more than the state of Louisiana. It contained present-day Louisiana and a dozen other states, totaling 2.1 million square kilometers. To be fair, the final price tag was more than $23 million, including interest. So, add a garage to your river-view unit in Shanghai.

Speaking of getting into the market at rock-bottom prices, New York's Manhattan was purchased in 1626 from native Americans for $24 worth of traded goods, or the equivalent of $500-700 in today's currency, according to an Oregon State University study of conversion.

And Alaska was purchased from Russia in 1867 for $7.2 million. And then oil squirted out from the frozen tundra.

Is there a theme here? A business paradigm for future generations of real estate investors? The founding buyers of America – oops, I mean the founding fathers – were really onto something big: They bought low and held tight – a strategy sneered at by day traders but exalted by old-fashioned tycoons like Warren Buffet.

But the lesson might have come too late for people like me, who missed out on the real estate boom either in China or elsewhere. Some years ago, I was tempted by the sale of one square inch of land somewhere in the United States.

Just as I thought that palm-size plot might one day turn into the next Manhattan, the same peddler started to offer moon property. A celestial commute would be oh-so-cool. I think I'll invite Superman to come to my New Year's party on the Milky Way next year. And I'll talk him into turning back the time so I can buy a state for the nifty price of a Shanghai apartment.

91. Dance of the catkins

May 11, 2007

The season of willow catkins is almost gone, and I'm starting to miss it.

For the past several weeks, those of us who live in Beijing have been bombarded by media accusations that these flying, dancing, gyrating cotton-ball-like clusters are the biggest nuisance of the all-too-short spring season in the city. They exacerbate asthma and clog auto parts, among other sins.

Being a good contrarian, I'll count the ways that willow catkins are good for the humankind. It's not an effort at balanced reporting – just another perspective.

As a starter, willow catkins are visually romantic. To save space, I won't quote you any of the immortal poems that our ancestors wrote to extol the unisexual apetalous flowers. But lovers walking on a sidewalk with thousands of soft balls floating around them make for a sight to kill for. If I were Gene Kelly, I'd do a number called "Singin' in the Catkins" and I'd kick up a whirlwind of catkins so that there will be cross-pollination of every character in the show.

As a matter of fact, filmmakers can find a variety of applications for such a scene. They can create a romantic gauze effect without resorting to soft focus lens. Say you are on a tight budget and cannot afford renting snow machines, catkins can be a passable substitute. If you want heavy snows, you can have the extras shake the willow trees.

Catkins floating on the street can also be put to good use. They are soft and tend to roll into bigger globs. That means, given a critical mass, they can function as a life-saving cushion for anyone jumping off tall buildings. Before the police arrive to rescue the migrant worker who threatens to plunge to the pavement to get his pay back, we can use brooms to gather enough catkins to create a pad of protection. And we'll call up the local television station and say: "Mr. DeMille of the DV generation, we are ready for close-up!"

They can be props for scientific experiments, too. When winds whip up a column of catkins, it is basically a tornado at play, though with much reduced force. We should take school children out on the street and have them observe the phenomenon.

I bet it'll elicit more wows than showing the movie *Twister*. Call it Meteorology 101, the field trip.

Speaking of science, catkins take a lot of explaining – why they are single sex and yet carry pollens from one sex to another. If that's too boring, we can dissect the sociological ramifications. The unisexual nature of catkins has blossomed into a vibrant human craze. Turn on the TV for any contest show, and you'll see the single-sex look of today's young.

Scientists have suggested removing catkins by injecting something into the willows and changing their sex. Such tampering has obviously pollinated the human species. For those contestants who dazzle with their androgynous appeal, I propose they don a catkin costume and do a catkin dance. If they can be as graceful, they'll have my vote.

92. The age of flaunting

May 23, 2007

If you've got it, flaunt it. In China, "it" more often than not refers to wealth.

Take a look at the giant outdoor billboards, and you'd be forgiven to believe that China is populated by 1.3 billion Bill Gates or mini-Gates.

There is nothing new about the current controversy about advertisers catering to the so-called "super-rich". We Chinese are so obsessed with the lifestyles of the rich and famous that the ultimate symbol of success is to live like them.

A decade ago, I was lured to make a television sitcom by a real estate developer. He wanted the show to promote his project in Beijing's northern suburb. You can call it a product tie-in because he proposed to title the show *Wealthy Village*.

I was driven there for location scouting. Surprisingly, it was row after row of townhouses, shoddily built and without any character or style. I doubted the genuinely rich would be interested, but those who wanted to be taken as one might have been impressed. In China, the eternal paradox is, the super rich tend to keep a low profile while those who have made wealth show-off into a low-brow art are usually miles away from the league of the super rich.

Thomas Friedman says that "middle class" is a state of mind. In China, affluence can also be a state of mind, especially when aided by such conspicuous displays as name-brand automobiles and clothes.

However, you shouldn't blame the wealth aspirants and new achievers. They are not called "nouveaux riches" for nothing. Poverty could be so traumatic that one is scarred for life and only by bathing oneself in the ointment of perceived opulence would he be able to remove the odor of the bad old days.

That is a dream come true for vendors who fatten their profit margins by positioning even run-of-the-mill products and services at high-end. If a fast-food restaurant promoted itself as the Western equivalent of a noodle shop or porridge stall, it wouldn't be able to suggest that eating a lot of burgers would somehow lead to Harvard success and billionaire happiness.

The more a business is known for championing lifestyle, the more it can charge a premium to the relentlessly upward mobile. To make it easier, lifestyle does not necessarily equal good taste.

There is a similarity between the Chinese fascination with money and the American fixation on size. In America, "small" for a piece of clothing is labeled "large", "medium" becomes "extra large", and "large" is enlarged to "extra extra large". We should perhaps adopt a similar strategy: A condo of 50 square meters is for the "rich", one of 100 for the super rich, and one of 200 for the super duper rich, and so on.

I suggest we outlaw the use of "affordable" in advertising. In its place, we should use "exorbitant".

For example, "our product is so exorbitant in pricing that it will take ten years of your income". If the consumer can buy it with two years of his income, he'd think he is five times better-heeled than the national average.

Middle class? Who wants to be stuck in the middle?

93. Arrested in Hong Kong – almost

June 07, 2007

Ten years ago, I visited Hong Kong for the first time. I was on my way home from New York and was dressed like a typical "boy in the 'hood". As soon as I was deposited onto a street corner at Central, I was stopped by a couple of cops. Having learned to lock valuables in the hotel safe, I could not produce my passport, but I squeezed out my best-possible Cantonese to explain my dilemma.

Unbeknownst to me, I was committing all the faux pas at once. The baggy jeans look had not spread to Asia yet, so I must have seemed like a country bumpkin who could not even afford a regular pair of torn jeans. And my Cantonese screamed, "This guy is from the mainland!"

As a matter of fact, the cops whispered to each other that I must be from Hainan Province, because my Cantonese was so awkward, I couldn't be from the Pearl River Delta. They turned to me and threatened: "Didn't you illegally emigrate here? If so, we'll repatriate you!"

I was relieved, and told them: "Go ahead. You'll save me the cost of a train ticket."

Afterward, I called up my friend and told him about the incident. He said, "It's not funny. You could get in trouble. You'd better speak English next time."

Sure enough, shortly afterwards, I was stopped again. Heeding my friend's advice, I pretended I did not know a word of Chinese. That really puzzled the Ah Sirs, as cops were known in the soon-to-be SAR of the PRC, and they struggled with their English.

"What do you mean I have to carry my passport? I can leave it with whomever I want. It's my right!"

That day, I was stopped three times by Hong Kong police. I must have looked really out of place.

Five years later, I was shuttling between Hong Kong and Guangzhou on a regular basis. I tried a variation of languages, including bad Putonghua, and nobody gave me the look any more.

On the contrary, whenever I arrived in Guangzhou, I'd notice migrant youths being stopped and checked for ID. I would walk right up to the semi-cops, but they'd never bother me. I thought it was strange, because the young men they harassed were dressed in their Sunday best, while I looked fresh off the boat, dragging my un-LV suitcase and sweating all over.

I told a lawyer friend of mine that I subconsciously wanted to be arrested – for being an outsider.

Why should I present my ID to them? If I were arrested for not having a local residency permit, I'd use the chance to do some investigative reporting, and my friend would come to bail me out.

"But you have to know, bad things might happen before I can get to rescue you at the detention center," she pointed out. Then, she described the kind of things she had seen there.

I think she was just scaring me.

I don't understand why Guangzhou cops saw me through and correctly marked me as a city resident. In New York, even Chinese shop owners took me for a Korean. Maybe I should say I'm from Henan and see how Beijingers react.

94. **My notebook died**

July 05, 2007

Unlike the golden hues shimmering in Richard Strauss' *Four Last Songs*, the golden years of a computer are not pretty.

My Sony Vaio notebook is on its deathbed. The first signal flared up a few months ago when it shut itself off without warning. Thinking the culprit must be a bad power connection combined with the drastically shortened life of the battery, I didn't cry my way to tech support.

In recent weeks, the frequency of sudden death is picking up. I still harbored the illusion that it could be a virus running amok until the master IT physicians ruled it out and zeroed in on the motherboard.

My Sony-san is four years old, which translates to 60 in human years. But I have to add another 20 years for making it toil for 10 hours a day. There are blots of smudge on the silvery cover. The palm rest has darkened to the point that it looks like the skin of a coal miner. Even the labels on the bottom have curled up into teeny-weeny rolls as if nature has been playing with them like a mischievous kid.

I would have preferred a desktop if I wasn't so into playing the intrepid reporter filing stories from the top of a karst mountain in southern China or a cruise liner that I suspect could be targeted by fun-phobic terrorists. My Sony has been with me through thick and thin.

I love my Sony. (Mr. Ryoji Chubachi, whom I interviewed last year, please give me credit if you decide to use it as your ad slogan.) It is slim, with the figure of a ballerina. Yet it packs a wallop, with plenty of power to sustain my heavy-duty word processing and – well, mostly word processing and storing digital photos and video clips of my daughter. (I didn't even venture into video editing.)

For full disclosure, it had an organ transplant at a young age. Just one year on my watch, it flashed a warning that its hard drive might be aging. Fearing data loss, I replaced it. Other than that, it did not give me any trouble, like a concubine who pushes all the right buttons.

My previous notebook was a Compaq, which I cannot describe in feminine terms. It was bulky and unreliable. I'd have to gain 80kg to make it compatible on my desk.

Before that was another American brand, which met its maker's maker even faster.

I've owned or used half a dozen notebooks in my life. I was with a computer magazine in Silicon Valley before I joined China Daily, so I could play with virtually any new model I wanted. My virgin notebook was an Apple. It looked sleek and mysterious, but it ran into fits of temper after only a few months with me, as if I had married a drug addict who had hidden all her symptoms from me.

Finally, it dawned on me that a notebook computer is like a pet hamster. No matter how much fun it gives you, it's gonna die on you. So, don't cry for me, Vaiovina.

95. Leaving a trail of dim sum like Hansel's trail of breadcrumbs

June 29, 2007

Tony Bennett left his heart in San Francisco. As a 12-year San Franciscan, I tend to leave something else of mine behind in every city I visit.

No, it's not what you think, you dirty mind. I always leave a little food in the hotel fridge whenever I travel to another city. It's a quirk I have demonstrated time and again. Just this week, I tried to avert my fate by resisting putting my food in the fridge in a Shanghai hotel. But on the morning I checked out, it occurred to me that I should not leave food around when I go outside and shut off the air-conditioner. So, I moved it to the fridge, making both a mental note and a physical one on a newspaper.

Sure enough, as soon as I was out of the city, I remembered what I had forgotten. I have always been meticulous and check every nook and crook of the room, but somehow, it never dawns on me to open the fridge.

What I bequeath to the hotel is not of much value. Usually, it's something like a few snack bars and some Chinese dim sum.

Strangely, I don't have a tendency to indulge in food binges and rarely eat anything after dinner. But the thought of having something handy is comforting. And I don't want to run up a 30-kuai bill for a chocolate bar that sells for 3 kuai in a supermarket – hence, my habit of lugging a little food in my suitcase.

I cannot make sense out of this ostensible contradiction. So, I conjured up my inner Freud and did a little self-psychoanalysis, which I then fused with Buddhism.

I was born shortly after famine struck the country in the early 1960s. It would be chronologically reasonable to assume that in my previous incarnation, I probably starved to death. I do not remember experiencing hunger or anything remotely like it. But here I am, with this irrational fear of it.

It's painful for me to attend Chinese banquets, because I have to witness large amounts of food thrown away. I was taught not to waste food. Before the American practices of using doggy bags and licking your fingers clean of any remnants of food were introduced to China, I was propounding them, eliciting sneers from friends.

When I was a kid, my mom used to tell me a fable about a wealthy family discarding great quantities of food day after day. The poor neighbor designed a way of "recycling" what was frittered away. One day, the rich family went bankrupt. And the poor man led him through a dark tunnel, which opened to a courtyard that glittered with gold. "This is how I turned your throwaways into fortune," he said.

I didn't know how it was done. Without any knowledge of chemistry, I thought leftover food could somehow morph into gold nuggets. Now, I would assume the neighbor could have been a pig farmer or something.

Sometimes, I wonder what would go through the mind of the cleaning lady when she finds my edible mementos. She'd probably think: "Is this supposed to be a tip or a scheme to make me fat?"

In the end, perhaps this article is a psychobabble defense mechanism to justify my own growing weight.

96. A tip for conversation etiquette

February 24, 2006

It is an experience many Westerners in China are familiar with: First it was a friendly "hello", then it snowballed into an avalanche of undesired greetings and an insistence on speaking English that borders on the psychotic, even if you speak only German or Portuguese.

What is wrong with these people, you may ask. Is China overrun by an army of overeager language learners with no knowledge of proper etiquette?

Well, first of all, those people did not heed their mothers' advice of "Don't talk to strangers."

As a matter of fact, we Chinese don't run around saying hello to strangers. We are traditionally withdrawn, nodding to acquaintances and asking "Have you eaten?" without expecting an honest answer or any answer at all.

But we are taught that people from the West are extremely open and friendly and we should show our hospitality by reciprocating in whatever level of English we have mustered. For many of us, that amounts to "Hello" and "Where do you come from".

You could have answered "I'm from that country somewhere near the Alps" if you didn't want to reveal your country of origin. You could even have said "Brokeback Mountain" without specifying whether you're from Wyoming, Montana or Canadian Alberta, but damn it, the popularity of the movie has ruined the obscurity for you.

Americans greet strangers while jogging in their own neighborhood, but they don't do so while ambling in a shopping mall. This may seem natural to an American, but hey, Miss Manners has not opened a course at Peking University, so it may be harder for us to grasp such a fine point than pick up a new language.

My advice to Westerners: if you don't want overzealous language students to harass you, avoid places like "English Corner" and restrict your conversation to "Hello" and "Goodbye". Dropping hints of ending an already long conversation is like asking an official to make a concise public speech. Any

On a deeper level, when normally reticent people turn into chatterboxes, it could mean one of several things: It could mean they are innately friendly but just don't know how to express it properly; it could also mean you have the potential to become a good shrink. See, they trust you. The downside? You won't get paid for it. Many visitors see it as a learning experience, and you can always turn the tide around in your favor and hone your Chinese language skills instead or play the globe-trotting journalist by firing a barrage of questions.

polite language would be too subtle.

When you settle down and work in a Chinese *danwei* as an expat, you may have colleagues come to you and pour their hearts out about every detail from office politics or sibling rivalry. That is when your status is elevated from shrink to confidant. Your big nose and blue eyes make you an outsider and thus an impartial third party. If you relay these gripes to another Chinese colleague, you'll be betraying the trust of a soul mate and losing the qualifications of an international mediator, so to speak.

Some foreign visitors complain about too many Chinese approaching them with chats that are too long. Normally, it's the visitors who are in a position to modulate the conversation. Of course they're too polite to cut it short since they feel they are essentially strangers in a strange land and don't want to commit any cultural faux pas. If worse comes to worst, such as when you bump into someone as garrulous as one of those old English ladies portrayed in films, you can either put up or shut up. By "shut up", I mean you play the shy and uncommunicative person so that the talker may feel you're unworthy of his or her time.

97. Bei-jingle bells ring in my kind of Christmas

December 25, 2007

I've always seen Christmas as the Western equivalent of Chinese New Year or Spring Festival. Like most Chinese consumers, I'm able to mentally discard all the religious associations and go right to the fun part.

Before you give me the full rundown of the origins of Christmas, I'll stake out my position: Both holidays take place at the end of a year, thus having the function of ringing out the old and ringing in the new; both feature family reunions complete with lavish banquets and gift giving; both highlight images that can happen only at the Northern Hemisphere, such as winter wonderlands and padded clothing.

In the true spirit of holiday frolicking, I'll combine the two occasions and come up with a very Chinese Christmas.

Santa Claus will embark on his journey in a grand sedan. The reindeers will be morphed into eunuchs, each holding a red lantern to light up the way. A crashing of the cymbal will announce the arrival of

Merry Christmas

the burly man. And of course, there's no way he'll climb down the chimney – that's so secretive and undignified.

The recipient family will be woken up and called into the front yard of their household, where the parents and their only child will kneel down and thank Santa for the precious gifts.

Santa will sing out the list of gifts to the tune of *Nessun Dorma*, accompanied by a Peking Opera orchestra. Given his size and shape, a baritone or a bass will probably look more suitable than a tenor.

That brings us to the issue of carols. The only Christmas carol popular in China is *Jingle Bells*, and it is sung at any time except December. You know why? Because bells stand out only in a quiet background. Let's change all the tinkling jingling bells into popping firecrackers.

That'll be very festively Chinese. And forget about *Silent Night*. Try *Noisy Night* instead. Now you know why I chose *Nessun Dorma*, which is Italian for "Nobody shall sleep".

I've heard an Afro version of Handel's *Messiah*, and that gave me a lot of inspiration. Yup, we should localize it to spread the message. The chorus should be replaced with a band of pipa, which will add to the urgency of the coming of baby Jesus. All those acrobatic vocals of coloratura can easily be transformed into Chinese opera, with higher pitches but without missing a beat.

Hallelujah can be performed while acrobats build a human pyramid, which is the ideal visualization of this endlessly upward-reaching piece of music.

Last but not least, the tree. It stays, but it has to be an orange tree – to symbolize good fortune. Instead of baubles, small oranges, real or plastic, will sparkle from the branches. Add to them couplets and riddles, and it'll last to the 15th day of the new year.

You'll never worry about toddlers gulping down inedible trinkets. If an ornament is not chewable, they'll automatically switch to a real orange. And every time you say "orange" in Chinese, the baby will say "Hey, you're blessing me with good luck!"

You see? A Chinese Christmas is not hard to imagine. And I bet *baijiu* makes perfectly intoxicating eggnog.

98. Haven for has-beens

Pop fans in China have a quirk.

They have this obsession with over-the-hill singers from the West. When I went to the States in the mid-1980s, Richard Marx was high on the billboard; and when I returned to China in the late 90s, "Right Here Waiting" was waiting for me on every radio dial in every city. And from where it stands, it's going to reverberate for another 10,000 years in karaoke heaven.

We're a people of nostalgia and our hit television talk show has made it a cult to parade celebrities from the golden age of the past. When it comes to foreign entertainers, we have treated every syrupy voice as the last straw and never learned to let go. Whitney Houston did not come here in the late 80s, when she reigned as the pop queen

supreme, but she showed her love for the Middle Kingdom in the new millennium when she had to take four breaths to finish "And I-I-I-I-I-eee-yaa will always love you."

Even Pararotti chose to complete his farewell concert in China, when the voice of the King of

High C was a pathetic shadow of his former glorious self. And every newspaper praised his "artistry", totally ignoring that it was strictly a "Thanks-for-the-memories" event.

This is comparable to "the Barry Manilow syndrome" in the US. He who "wrote the song" has recently been doing everything to jumpstart his career and is reportedly moving to Las Vegas for good. The Sin City used to be the warehouse for has-beens in American pop. I'd say King Elvis would have lived longer had he discovered China, or rather, the China market of loyal fans stuck in a time warp.

The gap between a musical fad in the West and Chinese catch-up is about a decade, give or take. In the cases of Karen Carpenter and Marx, they're immortalized in the mausoleum of eternity and beyond. A hundred rock 'n' rollers smashing guitars would not scrape a single chip off these monuments.

We love catchy tunes with universal appeal, from an era we remember with fondness. We'll bear young singers delivering horrendous cover versions rather than sharpen our ears for something different. We'll take the kitschiest songs from a distinctly unhip era for being hip.

Of course, musical taste is like fashion. Your father's golden oldies are definitely a telltale sign of "They didn't have better songs during that time." But your grandfather's show tunes, like silent films, can ooze cool if heard in proper setting.

One of the discoveries I made in recent years is how well Zhou Xuan's melodies from the 1940s have endured the test of time. The Little Sparrows from the 2000s cannot hold a light to this giant of pop kingdom of old Shanghai. She was truly China's own Edith Piaf or Judy Garland.

But then, I'm a big snob when it comes to music. I can't stand the low-brow ditties, nor the middle-brow ballads. (Well, I used to devour them when I was younger and didn't know better.) I squirm to see my home country being used as a showcase for washed-up performers who want to scrap every corner for every penny.

But hey, why should I care? I'm not the one paying for their tours.

99. Curse of the white tile

July 07, 2006

China's growth can be measured in myriad ways, most of which are economic, such as GDP, per capita income, even the fuzzy "Green GDP".

But when I travel across this vast land, it's the visual signs that impart the straightforward or subtle signals. A few years ago, I was in an inland town that was supposed to be poor and isolated from the outside world. Out of nowhere walked by a bunch of youngsters, dressed in hip jeans and carrying that in-vogue stare, complete with dyed blond hair.

"Hey, they're more stylish than we are. And we're the ones from the bright lights, big city," I joked.

Trust me. They were not tourists. They spoke the local dialect.

That notwithstanding, the unmistakable yardstick for me is not how people dress in a place, but the presence of the white-tiled building. Usually, the first phase of "walking into the age of modernity" is to embrace this architectural style, if it can be so called.

In my childhood memory, white tiles were a fixture of hospitals. They always had this sanitized connotation as if blood could be squirted on them

but they could miraculously come clean in a second.

In the early days of the reform and opening-up, buildings whose exteriors were plastered with white tiles (sometimes with slight color variations) began to pop up in coastal towns, a sure sign of new affluence, or rather, overcoming poverty.

However, it didn't take me long to realize this is the most vapid form of architecture on the planet, and I'm no architectural connoisseur. There is not a trace of creativity in the way the tiles are placed, or their size and shape. They have such a non-descript pattern that even old cement or dirt on the floor looks like a Caravaggio by comparison.

Their greatest benefit, which is ease of cleaning, has been turned on its head because China hardly has a tradition of periodically scrubbing the exterior of buildings. So, white tiles have become the easiest façade to gather dust and dirt.

As a result, a tiled building ages much faster in comparison to structures fronted with other building material.

In the past decade, some people in coastal areas have woken up to the reality that these buildings can truly be eyesores. So, they are moving into the second phase of structural design, with more diversity. But in inland towns, you still see mountains of white tiles that have buried elegant structure or the pragmatism of Soviet design.

"I guess this is the standard Guangdong county town look, and the hinterland aspires to be just as prosperous. Why should tourists spend thousands of yuan to come here to gawk at ubiquitous white tiles?" I used to rationalize with the city planners there.

"To them, white tiles may represent wealth, and we cannot stop people from showing off their newly gained status," they explained. "And it may take them another decade to understand that preserving their traditional, often ethnic, architectural style is like raising a cash cow for the future."

Come phase two, they will discard white tiles as "the shallowness of the transitional period", something like refusing to remove the brand tags on clothes or sunglasses. Phase three may be characterized by a mass rebuilding of old-style architecture, which sometimes mutates to constructing fake historic buildings.

I live in a tiled apartment building in Guangzhou and I'm not often bothered by it.

The reason? When I'm indoors, I don't see the tiles. But when I peek outside the window and notice the streak of stain that has darkened the tiles right beneath the window, I know they will always be a blot. I tried in vain to scrub it.

So, when people ask for instructions to get to my home, I say: "It's the one that looks the oldest. Maybe someday this will become heritage. But for me it'll never be vintage. It's just damn dirty."

Afterword

A few years ago, an American reporter was interviewing a young Chinese aspirant for journalism. What do you understand about "freedom of journalism", he asked her.

"Writing whatever I want without any restriction."

He knew, as I – and most of us – do, that there is no such absolute freedom anywhere in the world. The difference is in degrees.

Professionalism, ethics, objectivity and fairness (as well as the risks of libel and defamation) are big hurdles for "saying whatever you want", especially in the print media. Of course, the same freedom is gravely abused in many online forums and BBS discussions, but that's another story.

The realm of commentary offers much more room for self-expression. In the old days, Chinese media sprinkled reporting with colorful adjectives that reflected personal views; nowadays, you find them only on the opinion pages. Even then, opinions have to be tempered.

It is a privilege to be writing a personal column in an established media organization like China Daily where the wide array of readership from around the world offers tantalizing prospects for subjects. My challenge has always been relevance: Will what I say touch a chord – or sow discord? What new perspectives can I bring to an old topic? What new topics can I pick to put in perspective?

Fortunately, this is a time when China is going through dramatic changes; and there has been plenty to write about. I'm willing to listen to both sides and absorb whatever is reasonable – not necessarily a virtuous trait where being contrary – just for the sake of being so – is de rigueur to make your presence felt in the online world.

I select topics that I feel I can muster the whole truth, and tackle from every conceivable angle. Whatever I articulate represents only my own opinion – never my colleagues' or any organization's. But I do keep China Daily's readers in mind. Through this column, I wanted my readers to know more about China – the good, the bad and the changing. Only when you know the whole picture can you get perspective.

With a few exceptions, this collection is of my columns from China Daily's opinion page. The last chapter is selected from a humor column on the paper's Lifestyle section or from its affiliated newspapers, which I try to distinguish from the more serious column.

So, did I get to say whatever I wanted? Not always. But enough to make me happy – and make many of my readers respond.

Acknowledgments

My gratitude goes first and foremost to Mr. Zhu Ling, without whose "discovery" I would be in a different field. I have never had any training in journalism – never taken a single course or read a single book on this discipline. The closest to my current job was my MBA education in the University of California at Berkeley, where I had to finish half a dozen papers each week. Mr. Zhu has trusted and inspired me to do my best in writing about a country at the best possible time in its course of history – a time of rapid economic growth and constant changes.

I thank Ravi Shankar, whom I have the good fortune to call my mentor, for his patience and guidance.

My heartfelt thanks also go to Zhu Yuan, Liu Shinan, Li Xing, Qu Yingpu, Tan Hongkai and all the other colleagues who have helped me with various aspects of my work. You have made sitting at a computer 12 hours a day such an excitement, at least less than boredom.

Zhang Yaoning, Luo Jie, Liu Yanfeng, Pang Li and Li Zhengming provided cartoons, enlivening my book, for which I'm very grateful.

Dustie Yang and Debasish Roy Chowdhury helped me come up with the title of the book. (X-Ray is the name of my very first column, which was started while I was still living in Silicon Valley.)

The efficiency manifested by Zhang Meijing, Jing Xiaomin and Zhang Hong of the Intercontinental Press was nothing short of amazing.

Last but not least, I want to thank Zhu Yinghuang, Ed Zhang, Zhou Li, Zhao Huanxin, Huang Qing, Kang Bing, Gao Anming, Huang Xiangyang, Sun Shangwu, Xing Zhigang, Zhang Yifan, Zhi Renzhong, Zou Hanru, Yuan Zhou and Li Ge for their kind encouragement.